BOOK

OF

SOLITUDE

孤獨，一個人的狂歡

尼采／卡夫卡／吳爾芙——等人合著

黃意雯——譯

目次

編序	孤獨,一種原始的情感	4
I.	沉默的關係,激情的空虛	8
II.	卻不懂得吶喊	66
III.	必須一意孤行	112
IV.	灼傷,被猜疑的目光	182
V.	說好一起寂寞	248

編序
孤獨，一種原始的情感

漫步在現今城市之中，即使寒風大作，伴隨著酸楚的飢餓感，都不如孤獨和寂寞來得痛苦。人們習慣戴上面具，在出門前。一派輕鬆地步出家門，沿路點頭、哈腰，為了工作而乞討。走在路上，人們禮貌地互相衝撞，都穿著大衣、戴著大禮帽，但不知怎地，就是看不清楚對方的輪廓。

不知何故，當我們隻身投入自己的世界，竟能得到溫暖及滿足；但身處狂歡派對中則有如旁觀，遙望眾人的訕笑，看著合群的自己而感到寂寞。

眼下的社會，孤獨已經不再是一種物理狀態──並非單指一人的狀態，而趨於一種心理感受。有這種感受的人，散落在各個角落，紛紛閃爍寂寞的燈號，像是螢火蟲，隔著黑暗的虛空求救、試圖溝通。

唯有靜下心來咀嚼這段時光，仔細地端詳，才能發現孤單所呈現的各種樣貌——它的美醜、明暗、冷熱，甚至評判它的善惡。可是，孤獨的種類有太多，好似口味迥異的各種茶，各自適宜在不同的氣氛品茗。誠然，唯有親嘗才能讓自己成為那位鑑賞家。

　　二十世紀最偉大的物理學家之一，愛因斯坦形容自己活在「那年少時痛苦萬分，而成熟年歲裡卻倍感豐饒甜美」的孤寂當中；而獨自遠離塵囂，長年深居於瓦爾登湖的梭羅，終日醉心於大自然，這段時光他寫出許多動人作品。梭羅認為獨處是有益身心的，並「從沒找到一個比獨處更適合為伴的朋友」。

　　當然，並非所有孤獨造成的痛苦，都必須昇華、進化成某種力量——從中得到體悟的前提是：寂寞、痛楚都必須足夠深刻。

　　飽受精神折磨的梵谷說道：「我的靈魂暗藏炙熱烈火，卻無人駐足取暖，旁人走過只瞧見一縷輕煙。」梵谷那無法被理解、也無人可理解的內心何其孤寂。他只能站在一旁，為了表達、或為了有所體認，對自己的輕如鴻毛的孤單冷眼旁觀。於此，最貼切的則莫過費茲傑羅所言：「生命中最孤寂的時刻，就是眼看自己的世界分崩離析，卻只能茫然地望著。」

有研究指出，「恐懼」與「慾望」是人類兩大原始情感。而在本書中，孤獨也扮演了人類原始情感的投射——「不被他人理解」的恐懼以及「希望被他人理解」的慾望。為了解決這個難題，人類為自己打造了許多設施、發明物，如咖啡廳、公園座椅，或是手機、書，這些工具都是為了讓人排解寂寞而生的。只不過，即使端莊地坐在咖啡店閱讀，或選擇在公園當個低頭族，都會漸漸失去療效。唯有正視自我原始的情感，才是真正的排解之道。

　　《孤獨，一個人的狂歡》選錄了逾五十位名家的一百二十多則文字，或長或短。

　　首章〈沉默的關係，激情的空虛〉描述人與人之間一段悲傷的緣分，這種關係皆存在於你我記憶中，而記憶中的我們，都曾被歡愉的氣氛排擠、拋棄；二章〈卻不懂得吶喊〉是所有關係最後所烙印下、耐人尋味的劇痛；三章〈必須一意孤行〉則展現了孤獨的神祕及蘊含其內的未知能量，成為書中歷史名家們那人生孤單的途程上，不可或缺的精神食糧；然而，即使領悟到孤獨強大的力量，人卻依然無法抵抗寂寞，它也許藏身在幽暗之處，甚至從四面八方襲來——四章〈灼傷，被猜疑的目光〉正寫出了他人有如針尖的漠視，無心地傷害了這些獨行者。

終章〈說好一起寂寞〉是在通過所有孤獨體悟之後，人們再次打開內心的一個歷程。

而無論往後孤獨與否，人都終將放下前行。此時的視野已經開拓，自然能發現身旁許多相同處境的朋友。

透過這些名家的深刻體會、精巧文字的引領下，我們穿越時空，宛若坐上無盡宇宙內一艘開往未知的太空船。

艙外一片虛無。你看，不明的星體、塵落閃動，但可別著急，這些文字能給我們寄託和理解。圍繞著漫天星斗，我們一同咀嚼文字，一意孤行；在靜謐的森林中，端望美麗湖水投映的自己而掉下眼淚。

眼下，過往和未來都不再重要，就讓我們一起孤獨。

1
沉默的關係，激情的空虛

All men's miseries derive from not being able to sit quiet in a room alone.

—— **Blaise Pascal** 1623–1662

孤獨,一個人的狂歡

人類所有的不幸都源自於無法在一個房間內靜坐獨處。

——布萊茲・帕斯卡

孤獨，一個人的狂歡

God, but life is loneliness, despite all the opiates, despite the shrill tinsel gaiety of "parties" with no purpose, despite the false grinning faces we all wear. And when at last you find someone to whom you feel you can pour out your soul, you stop in shock at the words you utter—they are so rusty, so ugly, so meaningless and feeble from being kept in the small cramped dark inside you so long. Yes, there is joy, fulfillment and companionship—but the loneliness of the soul in its appalling self—consciousness is horrible and overpowering.

—— **Sylvia Plath** 1932–1963 : *The Unabridged Journals of Sylvia Plath*

神啊，儘管有那些麻醉劑，儘管有那些刺激、華麗、充滿歡樂氣息卻毫無意義的「派對」，儘管我們臉上都戴著虛偽的燦笑，可是生命卻是孤寂的。而當你終於找到一個可以吐露心聲的對象時，你會因為驚訝於你所吐露之言而沉默，這些話長久以來都藏在你內心那窄小、狹隘的黑暗當中，它們如此過時，如此醜陋，如此無意義與微弱。是啊，當然還有歡樂、滿足與友情，可是靈魂的孤寂感在它自身駭人的自覺中，是可怕且難以忍受的。

──普拉絲《希薇亞‧普拉絲日記》

We have a mind pliable in itself; that will be company; that has wherewithal to attack and to defend, to receive and to give: let us not then fear in this solitude to languish under an uncomfortable vacuity.

—— **Michel de Montaigne** 1533–1592 : *Essais*

我們有個內在柔軟的心智,它將成為伴侶,它有必要的手段去攻擊與防禦、接受與給予。別讓我們因畏懼孤獨,而在不安的空虛中枯萎凋落。

——蒙田《蒙田隨筆》

There was an emptiness about the heart of life; an attic room.Women must put off their rich apparel. At midday they must disrobe.

———**Virginia Woolf** 1882–1941 : *Mrs. Dalloway*

孤獨，一個人的狂歡

生命之心有一處空白，一間閣樓的房間。女人必須脫下她們的華服美衣。在白天，她們則必須脫下外衣。

——吳爾芙《達洛維夫人》

孤獨，一個人的狂歡

BOOK OF SOLITUDE

And you should not let yourself be confused in your solitude by the fact that there is something in you that wants to move out of it.

—— **Rainer Maria Rilke** 1875–1926 : *Letters to a Young Poet*

孤獨,　一個人的狂歡

在你的孤獨中，你不該因為自己體內那呼之欲出的某物而感到困惑。

—— **里爾克**《給年輕詩人的信》

I and me are always too deeply in conversation: how could I endure it, if there were not a friend?

The friend of the hermit is always the third one: the third one is the float which prevents the conversation of the two from sinking into the depth.

——**Friedrich Nietzsche** 1844–1900 : *Thus Spoke Zarathustra*

孤獨，一個人的狂歡

我和自己總是對談得太過投入：如果那稱不上是友情，我該如何忍受寂寞？

隱士的朋友永遠都是第三人：第三人是用來防止那兩人身陷對談的浮木。

——尼采《查拉圖斯特拉如是說》

Friendship, according to Proust, is the negation of that irremediable solitude to which every human being is condemned.

——**Samuel Beckett** 1906–1989 : *Proust*

孤獨，一個人的狂歡

友誼，根據普魯斯特的說法，就是人類皆被判處、無法治癒的孤獨之刑的負面結果。

──貝克特《普魯斯特》

—Alone, quite alone. You have no fear of that. And you know what that word means? Not only to be separate from all others but to have not even one friend.

—I will take the risk, said Stephen.

—And not to have any one person, Cranly said, who would be more than a friend, more even than the noblest and truest friend a man ever had.

——**James Joyce** 1882–1941 : *A Portrait of the Artist as a Young Man*

「孤獨，相當的孤獨。你對此毫不畏懼，但你知道這個字的意思嗎？不僅是要跟所有人隔離，甚至連一個朋友都不能有。」
「我願意冒這個險。」史蒂芬說。
「而且你連一個不只是朋友、甚至是一個遠超過你所能擁有，最高貴、最真誠的朋友的人都不能有。」克蘭利說。

―― 喬伊斯《一個青年藝術家的畫像》

I find it wholesome to be alone the greater part of the time. To be in company, even with the best, is soon wearisome and dissipating. I love to be alone. I never found the companion that was so companionable as solitude.

——**Henry David Thoreau** 1817–1862 : *Walden*

孤獨，一個人的狂歡

我認為長時間獨處是有益的。跟同伴相處，就算是跟最棒的人，一樣很快就會覺得疲倦與浪費體力。我喜歡獨處，我從沒找到一個比獨處更適合為伴的朋友。

—— **梭羅**《湖濱散記》

In other people's company I felt I was dull, gloomy, unwelcome, at once bored and boring...

——**André Gide** 1869–1951 : *The Immoralist*

孤獨，一個人的狂歡

有他人為伴時，我覺得自己遲鈍、陰鬱、不受歡迎，同時無聊又無趣。

—— 紀德《背德者》

Every moment of life wants to tell us something, but we do not want to hear what it has to say: when we are alone and quiet we are afraid that something will be whispered into our ear and hence we despise quiet and drug ourselves with sociability.

——**Friedrich Nietzsche** 1884–1900 : *Unpublished Writings from the Period of Unfashionable Observations*

生命時時刻刻都想傳遞訊息給我們，但是我們不願傾聽它想說的話：我們害怕一些事情會趁著我們獨處與靜默，如低語般傳入我們耳裡；因此，我們蔑視寧靜，並以社交毒害我們自己。

—— 尼采《未出版文集》

We do not think, in the holy places; we think in bed, afterwards, when the glare, and the noise, and the confusion are gone, and in fancy we revisit alone, the solemn monuments of the past, and summon the phantom pageants of an age that has passed away.

——**Mark Twain** 1835–1910 : *The Innocent Abroad*

在神聖的地方，我們從不思考；我們只在床上思考，之後，當光芒、噪音和疑惑全消失後，在幻想中，我們獨自重訪從前那莊嚴的紀念碑，並召喚已逝年華那如幽魂般的盛會。

——馬克・吐溫《傻子旅行記》

I am now quite cured of seeking pleasure in society, be it country or town. A sensible man ought to find sufficient company in himself.

—— **Emily Brontë** 1818–1948 : *Wuthering Heights*

孤獨，一個人的狂歡

無論在鄉下或城市,我於社交圈中尋求快樂的症狀已幾乎被治癒了。一個有理智的人應該能從自身中找到足夠的陪伴。

──艾蜜莉・勃朗特 《咆哮山莊》

孤獨，一個人的狂歡

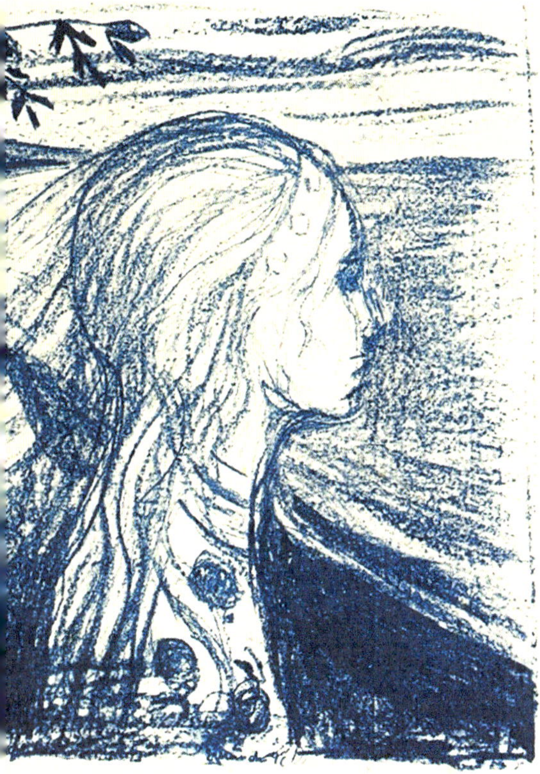

I want someone to sit beside after the day's pursuit and all its anguish, after its listening, and its waitings, and its suspicions. After quarrelling and reconciliation I need privacy—to be alone with you, to set this hubbub in order. For I am as neat as a cat in my habits.

——**Virginia Woolf** 1882–1941 : *The Waves*

孤獨,一個人的狂歡

在一日的追逐與它帶來的身心俱疲、聆聽、等待與懷疑之後，我想要有個人坐在我身邊。在爭執與和解之後，我需要隱私——跟你獨處在一起，讓所有的喧囂嘈雜井然有序。因為在我的習慣裡，我像貓一樣整潔。

——吳爾芙《海浪》

But then there's loneliness. However you might philosophise about it, loneliness is a terrible thing, my dear fellow... Although in reality, of course, it's absolutely of no importance!"

——**Anton Chekhov** 1860–1904 : *The Three Sisters*

孤獨, 一個人的狂歡

然而,還有寂寞。我親愛的夥伴,不論你如何將之哲理化,寂寞就是一件可怕的事⋯⋯當然了,雖然在現實中,它絕對一點兒都不重要!

——契訶夫《三姊妹》

Nowadays feeling alone fills me with appalling anguish; being alone at home, by the fire, in the evening. It seems to me then that I'm alone on the earth, dreadfully alone, but surrounded by indeterminate dangers, by unknown, terrible things; and the wall, which divides me from my neighbour, whom I do not know, separates me from him by as great a distance as that which separates me from the stars I see through my window. A kind of fever comes over me, a fever of pain and fear, and the silence of the walls terrifies me. It is so profound, so sad, the silence of the room in which you live alone. It isn't just a silence of the body, but a silence of the soul, and, when a piece of furniture creaks, a shiver runs through your whole body, for in that dismal place you expect to hear no sound.

——**Guy de Maupassant** 1850–1893 : *Bel-Ami*

近來，孤獨感以駭人的苦痛包圍我；我獨處家中，依偎著爐火，在入夜時分，我彷彿孤獨於世，極度地孤獨，卻又被不確定的危險、未知的可怕事物包圍；還有牆壁，分隔了我和我的鄰居，我不認識的鄰居，以從我的窗戶望向群星那樣的遙遠距離阻隔我和我的鄰居。一股灼熱感朝我襲來，混雜著痛苦與恐懼的灼熱，還有這四壁的寂靜驚嚇了我。你獨居的房間發散出的孤獨感如此深沉、如此悲傷。這不僅僅是肉體的寂靜，還是靈魂的寂靜，然而，當一件傢俱吱響出聲，一股震顫便傳遍你的全身，因為在如此晦暗之處，你並未預期任何聲響。

—— 莫泊桑《漂亮朋友》

It was a desire, an echo, a sound; she could drape it in color, see it in form, hear it in music, but not in words; no, never in words. She sighed, teased by desires so incoherent, so incommunicable.

—— **Virginia Woolf** 1882–1941 : *Night and Day*

孤獨，一個人的狂歡

那是一股慾望,一陣回音,一絲聲響;她可以用色彩裝飾它,在形體中看見它,從音樂中聽到它,但無法以言語,絕對不能以言語表達。她嘆了口氣,被如此不連貫、如此難以溝通的慾望嘲笑。

──吳爾芙《夜與日》

If you're lonely when you're alone, you're in bad company.

—— **Jean-Paul Sartre** 1905–1980

孤獨，一個人的狂歡

如果你隻身一人時會感覺寂寞，那表示你正處於惡劣的關係之中。

── 沙特

孤獨，一個人的狂歡

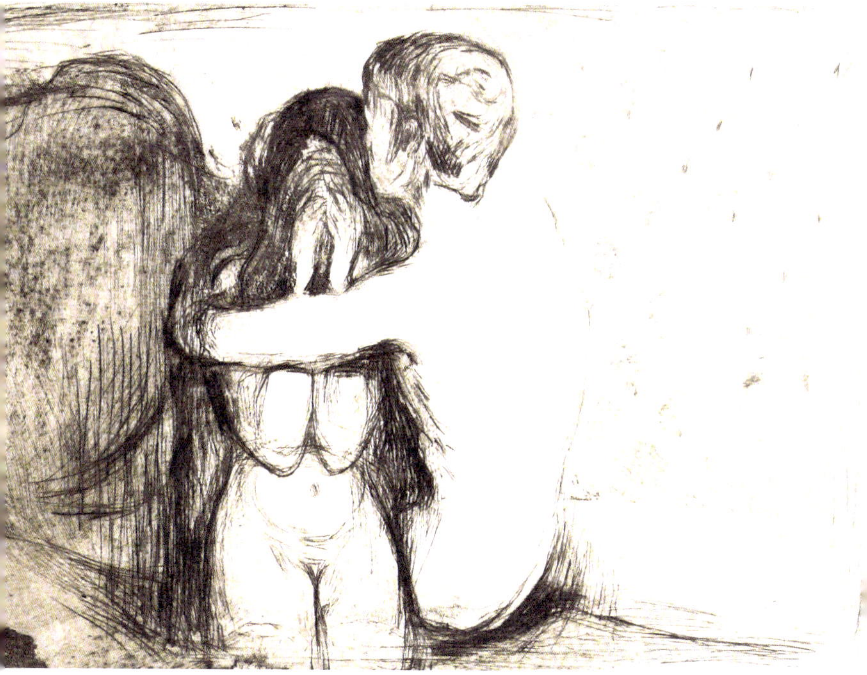

It is in your power to withdraw yourself whenever you desire. Perfect tranquility within consists in the good ordering of the mind, the realm of your own.

——**Marcus Aurelius** 121 –180 : *Meditations*

孤獨，一個人的狂歡

當你升起慾望之際,你必須盡全力抽離自身。內在完美的寧靜存在於端正不息的心智 —— 你自身的領域。

—— 奧里略《沉思錄》

There is only *one* solitude, and it is vast, heavy, difficult to bear, and almost everyone has hours when he would gladly exchange it for any kind of sociability, however trivial or cheap, for the tiniest outward agreement with the first person who comes along....

——**Rainer Maria Rilke** 1875–1926 : *Letters to a Young Poet*

孤獨，一個人的狂歡

只有一種孤獨，它巨大、沉重、難以忍受，而且幾乎每個人都曾有那麼片刻，樂意以之交換任何形式的社交，不論何其瑣碎或廉價，都是為了和第一個前來的人，做出那微不足道、且流於形式的約定。

── 里爾克《給年輕詩人的信》

She had known happiness, exquisite happiness, intense happiness, and it silvered the rough waves a little more brightly, as daylight faded, and the blue went out of the sea and it rolled in waves of pure lemon which curved and swelled and broke upon the beach and the ecstasy burst in her eyes and waves of pure delight raced over the floor of her mind and she felt, It is enough! It is enough!

—— **Virginia Woolf** 1882–1941 : *To the Lighthouse*

孤獨，一個人的狂歡

她曾懂得快樂，細微的快樂，強烈的快樂，而這些快樂為洶湧的海浪增添了一點明亮，當天光褪去，從海中升起的那抹藍色，捲入淡黃的海浪中，捲起、膨脹，最後碎裂在海灘上，這分狂喜在她眼中爆發，純粹的喜悅之浪溢過她的理智，她想著：夠了！夠了！

──吳爾芙《燈塔行》

Solitude is fine but you need someone to tell you that solitude is fine.

——**Jean-Louis Guez de Balzac** 1597–1654 : *Dissertations chrétiennes et morales*

孤獨，一個人的狂歡

孤獨是件好事,但你需要有人告訴你,說孤獨是件好事。

—— 尚路易‧貴茲‧德‧巴爾札克《基督教及道德文集》

Smoking is indispensable if one has nothing to kiss.

——**Sigmund Freud** 1856–1939 : *Letter January 22, 1884*

孤獨，一個人的狂歡

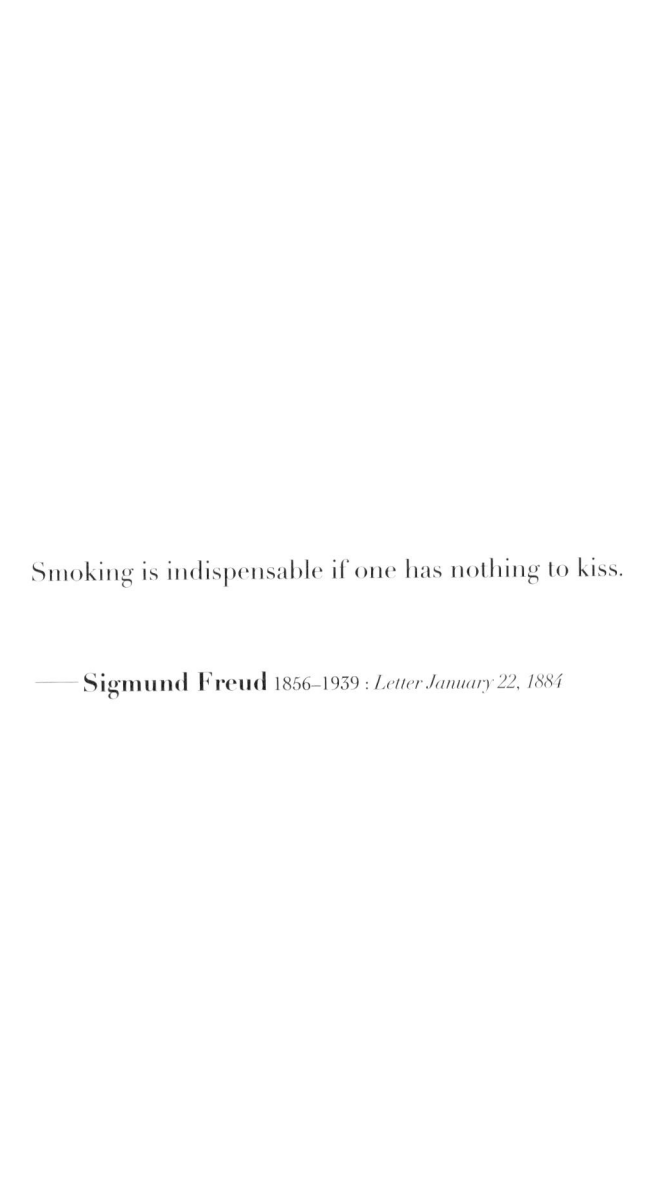

抽菸是必要的,如果你無人可吻。

——**佛洛伊德**一八八四年一月二十二日信件

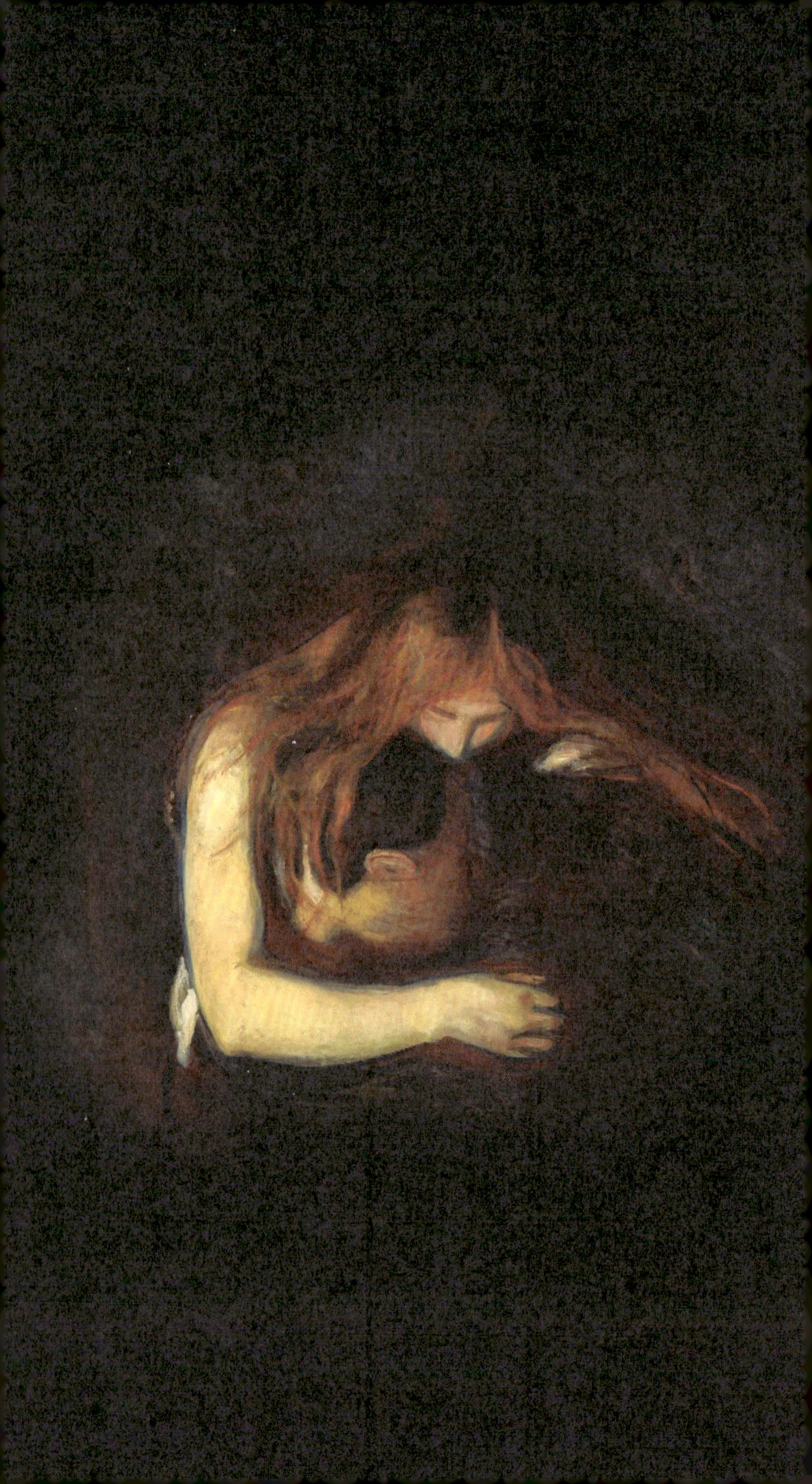

II

却不懂得呐喊

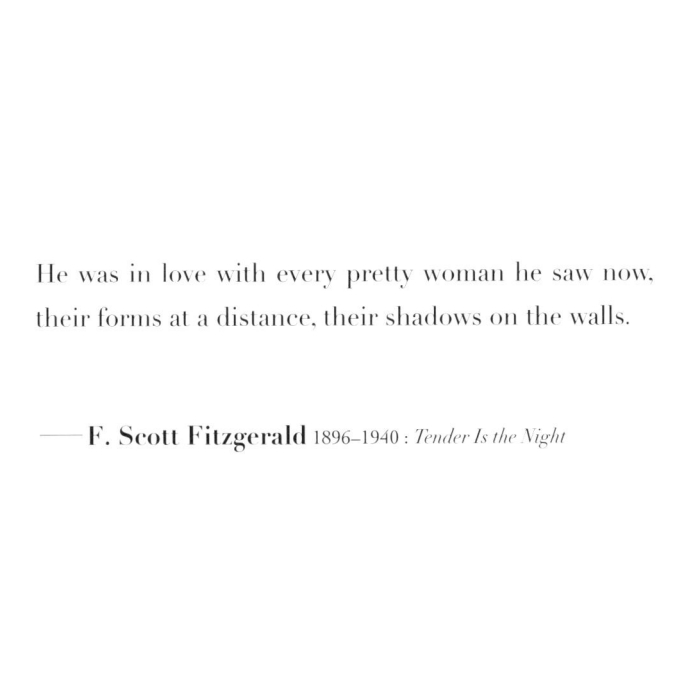

He was in love with every pretty woman he saw now, their forms at a distance, their shadows on the walls.

——F. Scott Fitzgerald 1896–1940 : *Tender Is the Night*

孤獨，一個人的狂歡

他愛上了放眼所及的每個女子,她們的軀體在遠方,而身影映在牆上。

──費茲傑羅《夜未央》

...here you used to be, there is a hole in the world, which I find myself constantly walking around in the daytime, and falling in at night. I miss you like hell.

——**Edna St. Vincent Millay** 1892–1950 : *Letters of Edna St. Vincent Millay*

孤獨，一個人的狂歡

從前你所在之處,有個洞在這世上,我發現自己白天時經常在附近走動,入夜則深墜其中。我對你的思念無可救藥。

──聖文森・米萊《書信集》

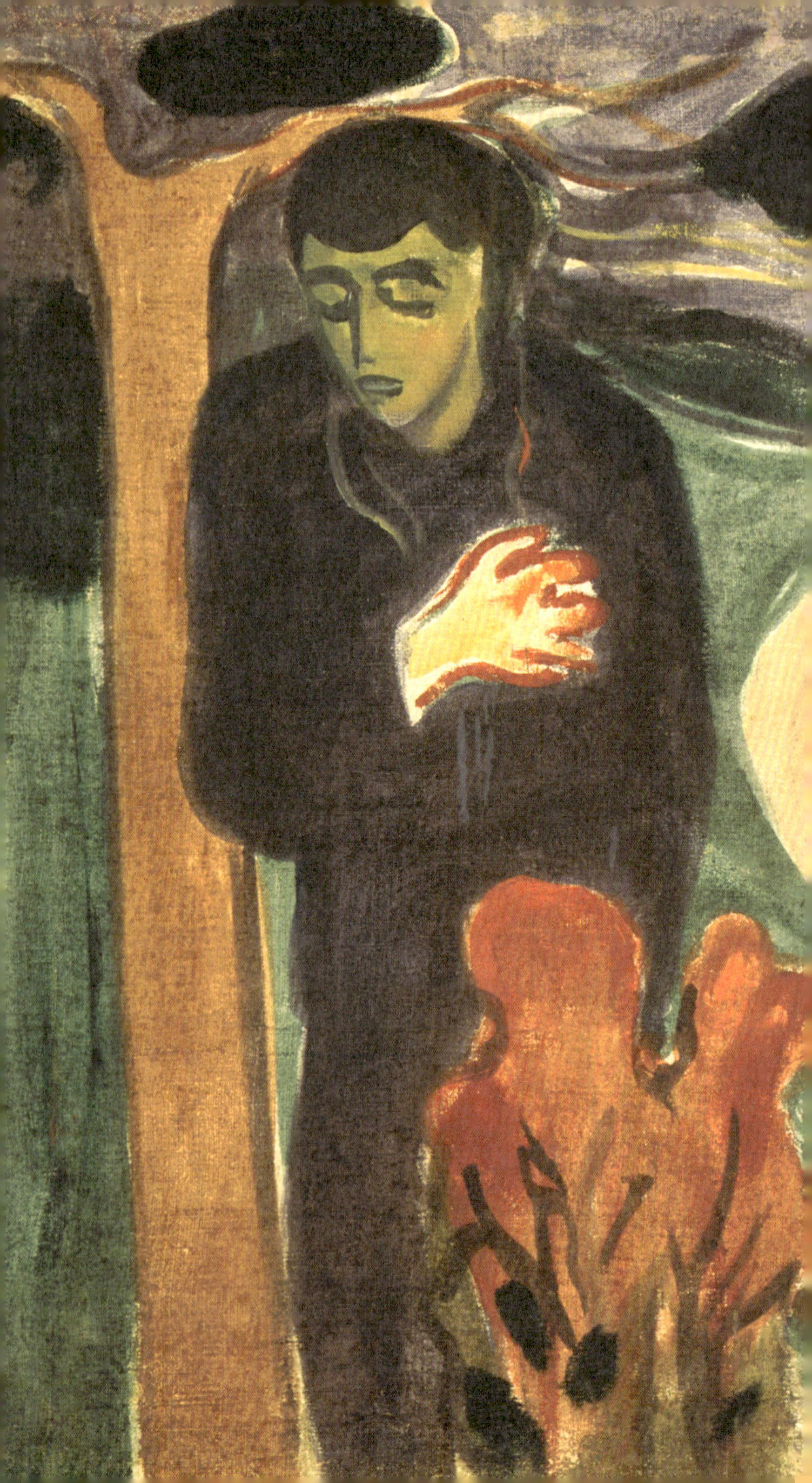

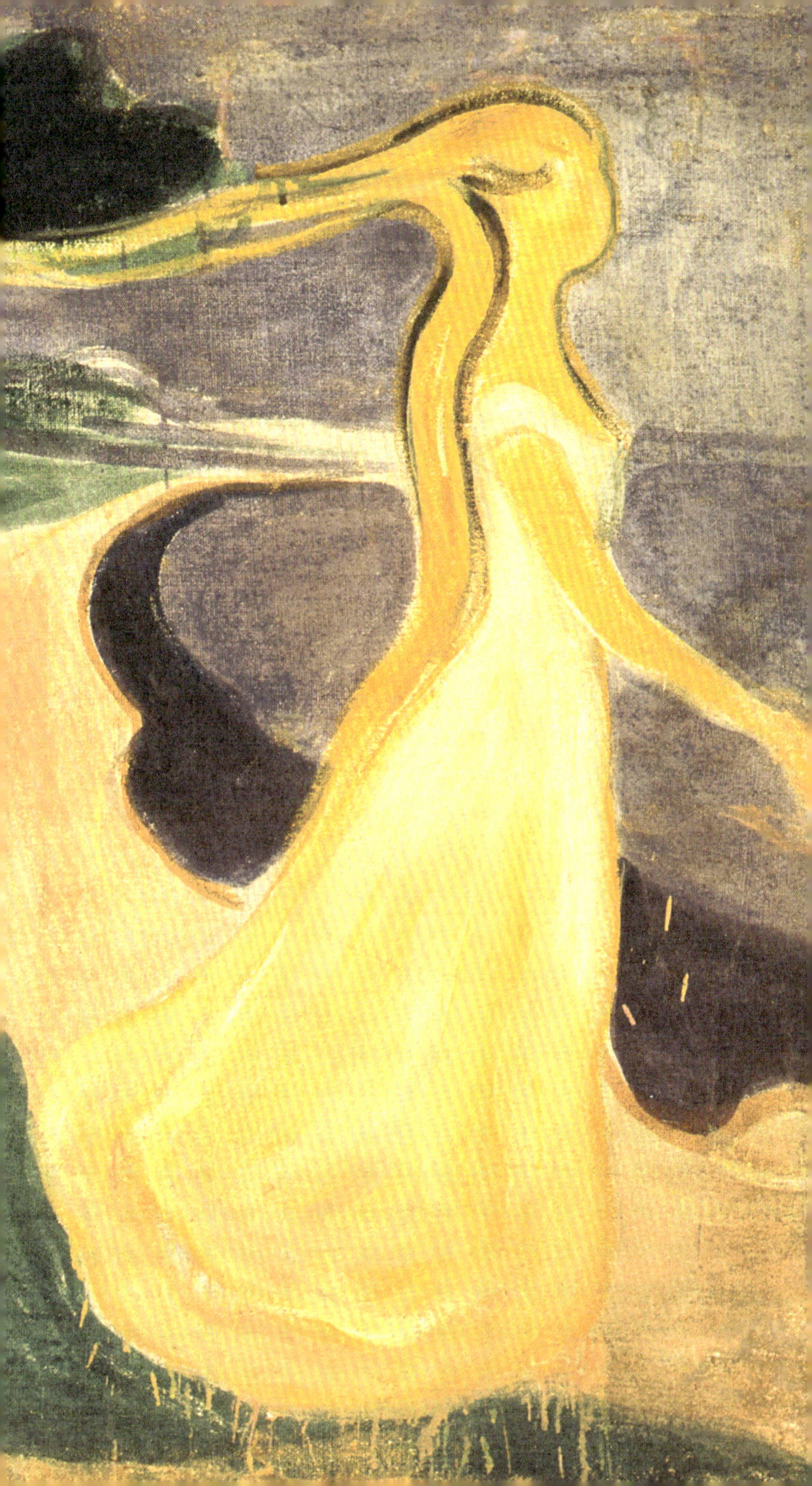

There are days when solitude is a heady wine that intoxicates you with freedom, others when it is a bitter tonic, and still others when it is a poison that makes you beat your head against the wall.

——**Colette** 1873–1954 : *Oeuvres complètes en seize volumes*

有時，孤獨好似一杯醉人美酒，以自由讓你陶醉；有時，它是苦澀的通寧水；而有時，它則是讓你想要一頭撞牆的毒藥。

―― **柯蕾特**《作品集六卷》

Solitude was my only consolation — deep, dark, deathlike solitude.

——**Mary Shelley** 1797–1851 : *Frankenstein*

孤獨,一個人的狂歡

孤獨是我唯一的慰藉 —— 深沉、幽暗、死亡般的孤獨。

—— 瑪麗・雪萊 《科學怪人》

Who, if I cried, would hear me among the angelic orders? And even if one of them suddenly pressed me against his heart, I should fade in the strength of his stronger existence. For beauty's nothing but the beginning of terror we're still just able to bear.

——**Rainer Maria Rilke** 1875–1926 : *Duino Elegies*

若我哭泣,在那些天使中,誰能聽見我的悲鳴?就算他們之中有人忽然將我按向他的心窩,我也會在他存在感強大的力道中凋謝。因為美只是我們尚且能隱忍之恐懼的前奏。

—— **里爾克**《杜伊諾哀歌》

I felt a haunting loneliness sometimes, and felt it in others—young clerks in the dusk, wasting the most poignant moments of night and life.

———— F. Scott Fitzgerald 1896–1940 : *The Great Gatsby*

孤獨, 一個人的狂歡

我有時候會感到一種難以排遣的寂寞，同時也在其他人身上感受到 —— 黃昏裡的年輕職員，揮霍夜晚和人生中最深刻的時光。

── **費茲傑羅**《大亨小傳》

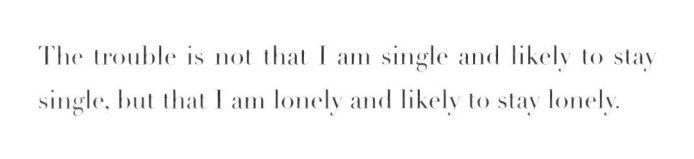

The trouble is not that I am single and likely to stay single, but that I am lonely and likely to stay lonely.

——**Charlotte Brontë** 1816–1855 : *attributed, Complete Novels of the Brontë Sisters*

問題不在於我單身，並很可能一直單身下去，而是我很寂寞，並很可能一直寂寞下去。

──夏綠蒂・勃朗特《勃朗特姊妹小說集》

I've never been in love. I've dreamt of it day and night, but my heart is like a fine piano no one can play because the key is lost.

—— **Anton Chekhov** 1860–1904 : *The Three Sisters*

孤獨，一個人的狂歡

我從未愛過。我曾日夜夢想著愛，然而，我的心猶如一架細緻的鋼琴，無人能彈奏，因為那琴鍵已遺失。

—— 契訶夫《三姊妹》

Solitude has soft, silky hands, but with strong fingers it grasps the heart and makes it ache with sorrow.

——**Kahlil Gibran** 1883–1931 : *The Broken Wings*

孤獨有雙如絲般柔軟的手,但它用有力的手指,掐著你的心,讓你的心與悲傷一起疼痛。

——紀伯倫《折翼》

孤獨，一個人的狂歡

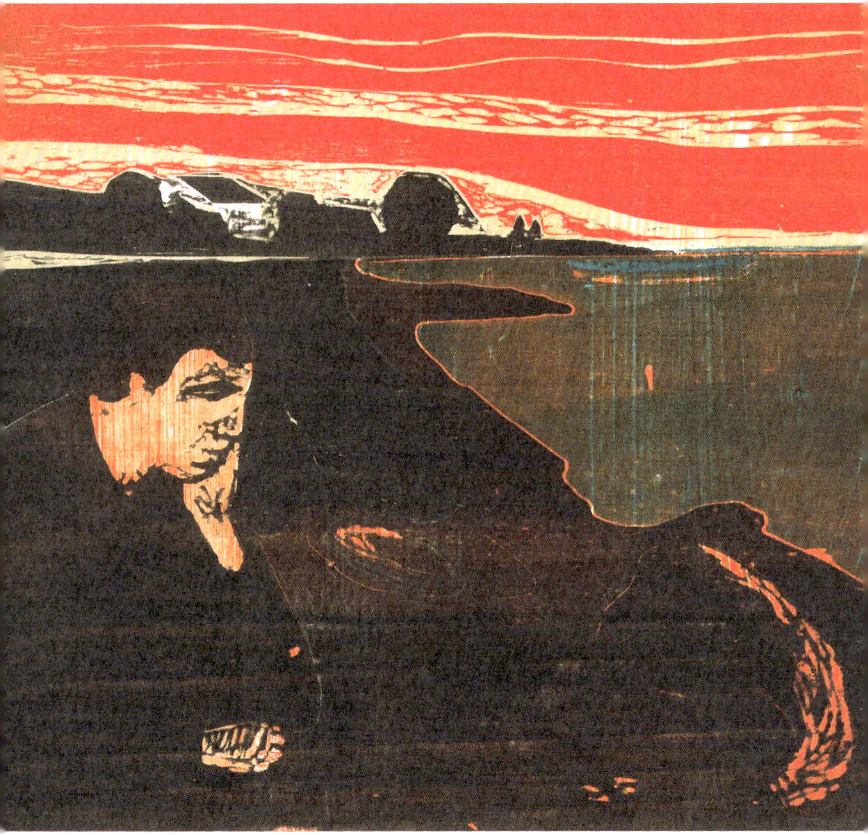

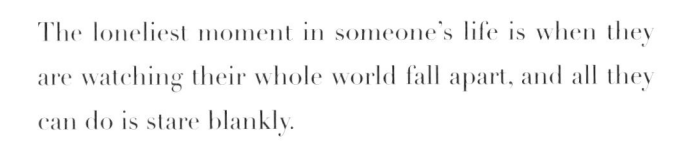

The loneliest moment in someone's life is when they are watching their whole world fall apart, and all they can do is stare blankly.

—— **F. Scott Fitzgerald** 1860–1940 : *The Great Gatsby*

孤獨，一個人的狂歡

生命中最孤寂的時刻，就是眼看自己的世界分崩離析，卻只能茫然地望著。

—— 費茲傑羅《大亨小傳》

I have absolutely no pleasure in the stimulants in which I sometimes so madly indulge. It has not been in the pursuit of pleasure that I have periled life and reputation and reason. It has been the desperate attempt to escape from torturing memories, from a sense of insupportable loneliness and a dread of some strange impending doom.

―― **Edgar Allan Poe** 1809–1849

在有時教我瘋狂沉溺的杯中物裡，我絲毫不覺一絲快感。我甘冒喪失生命、名譽和理智的風險，並非為了追求享樂。那是我試圖逃離的絕望之舉，逃離苦痛的回憶、難耐的孤寂，以及逃離對某種詭異厄運步步近逼的恐懼。

——愛倫坡

What is hell? Hell is oneself.
Hell is alone, the other figures in it
Merely projections. There is nothing to escape from
And nothing to escape to. One is always alone.

——**T.S. Eliot** 1888–1965 : *The Cocktail Party, Act1.Scene3.*

孤獨，一個人的狂歡

何謂地獄？地獄即是自身。

地獄是孤獨的，地獄裡的其他影像僅是投影。

無事需逃離，亦無事可往。人一直都是孤獨的。

―― T.S. 艾略特《雞尾酒派對》劇作第一幕第三景

I have heard the mermaids singing, each to each.
I do not think that they will sing to me.

—— **T.S. Eliot** 1888–1965 : *The Love Song of J. Alfred Prufrock*

我曾聽過美人魚唱歌,彼此對唱。

我不認為她們會對著我唱。

── T.S. 艾略特《J. 阿夫列德‧普魯芙洛克的情歌》

I have hardly anything in common with myself and should stand very quietly in a corner, content that I can breathe.

—— **Franz Kafka** 1883–1924

我和自己幾乎沒有任何共識,我應該安靜地站在角落,對自己竟還能呼吸感到滿意。

──卡夫卡

To forget a friend is sad. Not everyone has had a friend.

——**Antoine de Saint-Exupéry** 1900–1944 : *The Little Prince*

孤獨,一個人的狂歡

忘記朋友是件傷心的事。不是每個人都曾有過朋友。

──聖修伯里《小王子》

Are the dead as lonesome as the living?

—— **Truman Capote** 1924–1984 : *Other Voices, Other Rooms*

孤獨，一個人的狂歡

逝者和生者一樣寂寞嗎?

——卡波堤《其他聲音·其他房間》

Yes, in my life, since we must call it so, there were three things, the inability to speak, the inability to be silent, and solitude, that's what I've had to make the best of.

——**Samuel Beckett** 1906–1989 : *The Unnamable*

是的,在我的生命裡,既然我們必須如此稱呼它,有三件事情是我必須善加利用的:無法言語、無法沉默與孤獨。

―― 貝克特《無以名狀》

The more we speak of solitude, the clearer it becomes that at the bottom it is not something one can choose to take or leave. We are lonely. One can deceive oneself about it and act as if it were not so. That is all. But it is so much better to see that we are so, indeed even to presuppose it. It will make us dizzy, of course; because all the focal points on which our eyes were used to resting are taken away from us, there is nothing near us anymore, and everything distant is infinitely distant.

—— **Rainer Maria Rilke** 1875–1926 : *Letters to a Young Poet*

我們越是談論孤獨，它就越清晰，說到底，它並不是我們可以任意選擇帶走或留下的。我們都寂寞，你可以欺騙自己，裝成若無其事，但也僅能如此。然而，認清事實對我們更好，即使只是去做假設。當然，寂寞讓我們暈眩，因為我們雙眼曾凝視的焦點皆被剝奪而去，我們身邊再也沒有任何東西，而所有遙不可及之物，依然無盡地遙不可及。

—— 里爾克《給年輕詩人的信》

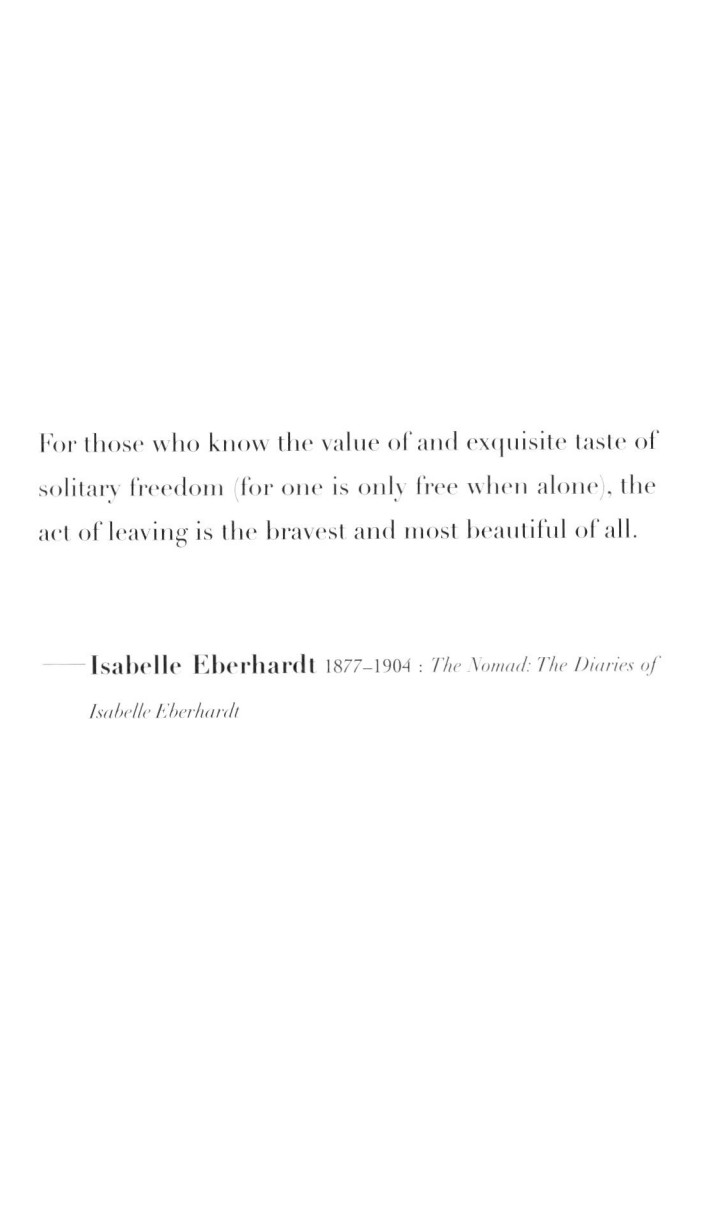

For those who know the value of and exquisite taste of solitary freedom (for one is only free when alone), the act of leaving is the bravest and most beautiful of all.

——**Isabelle Eberhardt** 1877–1904 : *The Nomad: The Diaries of Isabelle Eberhardt*

對那些懂得孤獨的自由（唯有獨處，人才真正自由）之可貴與絕妙滋味的人而言，離開，是最勇敢也是最美麗的行為。

──**伊莎貝爾・艾伯哈特**《遊牧民族：伊莎貝爾・艾伯哈特日記》

孤獨，一個人的狂歡

BOOK OF SOLITUDE

III
必須一意孤行

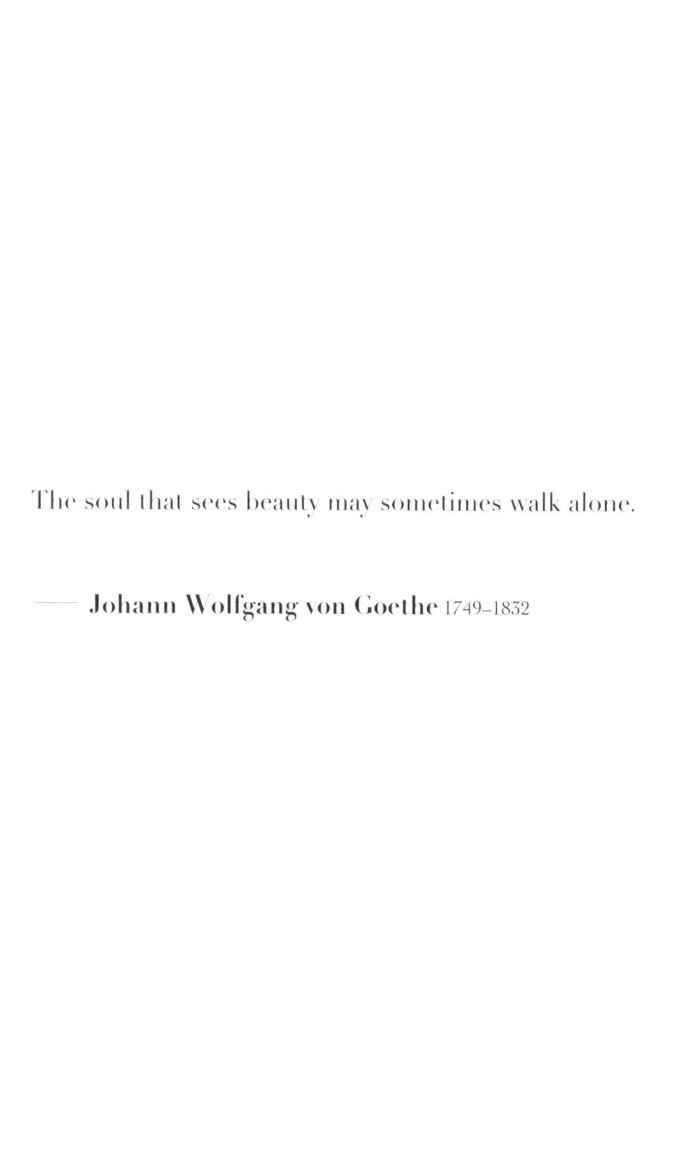

The soul that sees beauty may sometimes walk alone.

─── **Johann Wolfgang von Goethe** 1749–1832

孤獨，一個人的狂歡

看得見美的靈魂，有時可能踽踽獨行。

——歌德

Solitude is independence. It had been my wish and with the years I had attained it. It was cold. Oh, cold enough! But it was also still, wonderfully still and vast like the cold stillness of space in which the stars revolve.

—— **Hermann Hesse** 1877–1962 : *Steppenwolf*

孤獨，一個人的狂歡

孤單就是獨立。這一直是我的願望，這些年來我也達成了。它是冷冰冰的，噢，真夠冷的！然而它也是靜謐的，靜謐得如此美妙，而且一如繁星運行其中的冷寂宇宙那般浩瀚。

—— 赫塞《荒原狼》

The more powerful and original a mind, the more it will incline towards the religion of solitude.

——**Aldous Huxley** 1894–1963 : *Proper Studies*

孤獨,一個人的狂歡

越是有力、原始的心靈，就越發傾向追求孤獨。

—— 赫胥黎《Proper Studies》

I need to be alone. I need to ponder my shame and my despair in seclusion; I need the sunshine and the paving stones of the streets without companions, without conversation, face to face with myself, with only the music of my heart for company.

——**Henry Miller** 1891–1980 : *Tropic of Cancer*

我需要獨處。我需要在孤獨中反省我的恥辱與絕望。我需要無人同行的陽光與石板路,不需要任何對話,只與自己面對面,只有我心中的音樂為伴。

—— 亨利・米勒《北回歸線》

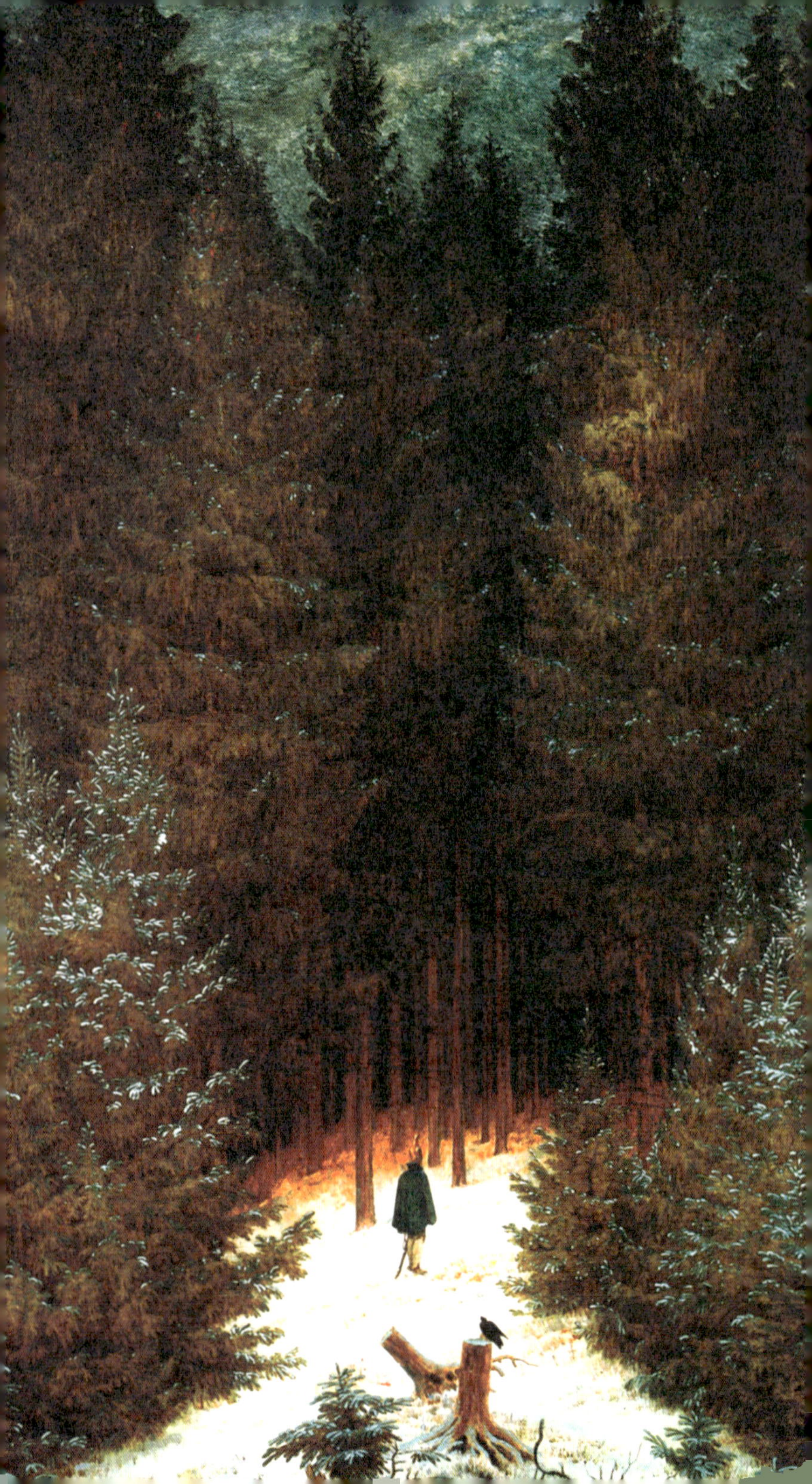

BOOK OF SOLITUDE

Two possibilities exist: either we are alone in the Universe or we are not. Both are equally terrifying.

———**Arthur C. Clarke** 1917–2008 : *provided by Neil McAleer, Arthur C. Clarke's biographer,*

有兩種可能性存在：我們要不就是全然地孤獨於世，要不就不是。這兩者同樣駭人。

──亞瑟・克拉克

This sometimes happened: from time to time, Dantès, driven out of solitude into the world, felt an imperative need for solitude. And what solitude is more vast and more poetic than that of a ship sailing alone on the sea, in the darkness of night and the silence of infinity, under the eye of the Lord?

—— **Alexandre Dumas** 1802–1870 : *The Count of Monto Christo*

孤獨, 一個人的狂歡

有時候，一個人孤伶伶在世上的唐泰斯不時會對孤獨感到強烈的需求。而什麼樣的孤獨會比一艘在上帝的看顧下、在暗夜的漆黑和無窮的寂靜中獨自航行海上的船隻，更顯浩瀚、更具詩意？

——大仲馬《基督山恩仇記》

We live as we dream—alone...

—— **Joseph Conrad** 1857–1924 : *Heart of Darkness*

孤獨,一個人的狂歡

我們活著，當我們獨自夢想之時。

―― 康拉德《黑暗之心》

How much better is silence; the coffee cup, the table. How much better to sit by myself like the solitary sea-bird that opens its wings on the stake. Let me sit here for ever with bare things, this coffee cup, this knife, this fork, things in themselves, myself being myself.

——**Virginia Woolf** 1882–1941 : *The Waves*

寂靜有多好；咖啡杯，桌子。像海鳥在木樁上孤獨展翅地獨坐著該有多好。讓我跟這些樸素的器物永遠坐在一起，這個咖啡杯、這把刀子、這隻叉子，事物皆回歸其本質，我自己做我自己。

—— 吳爾芙《海浪》

A man can be himself only so long as he is alone; and if he does not love solitude, he will not love freedom; for it is only when he is alone that he is really free.

——**Arthur Schopenhauer** 1788–1860 : *Essays and Aphorisms*

孤獨，一個人的狂歡

唯有獨處，人才能做自己；人如果不愛孤獨，那他也不會喜愛自由，因為只有獨處時，他才是完全的自由。

—— 叔本華《散文與箴言》

Tea should be taken in solitude.

——**C.S. Lewis** 1898–1963 : *Surprised by Joy: The Shape of My Early Life*

孤獨，一個人的狂歡

孤獨適宜品茶時服用。

—— C.S. 路易斯《因喜悅而驚喜：我的早年生活》

孤獨，一個人的狂歡

Our language has wisely sensed these two sides of man's being alone. It has created the word "loneliness" to express the pain of being alone. And it has created the word "solitude" to express the glory of being alone. Although, in daily life, we do not always distinguish these words, we should do so consistently and thus deepen our understanding of our human predicament.

—— **Paul Tillich** 1886–1965 : *The Eternal Now*

我們的語言聰明地感受到人類孑然一身的兩面。它創造了「寂寞」來表達獨處時的痛苦；也創造了「孤獨」來表達獨處時的狂喜。然而，在日常生活中，我們並不常區別這兩個詞彙，我們應該持續地區分兩者，以加深我們對人類處境的認識。

——田立克《永恆的現在》

I need solitude for my writing; not 'like a hermit' — that wouldn't be enough — but like a dead man.

——Franz Kafka 1883–1924

孤獨，一個人的狂歡

我寫作時需要保持孤獨,不是「像個隱士一般」;那遠遠不夠,而是像死人一樣。

──卡夫卡

It is a frightful satire and an epigram on the modern age that the only use it knows for solitude is to make it a punishment, a jail sentence.

——**Søren Kierkegaard** 1813–1855 : *Works of Love*

這真是現代駭人的嘲諷與警訊。孤獨,我們對它所知唯一的用途,竟是作為一種懲罰,一種牢獄之刑。

——齊克果《愛之工》

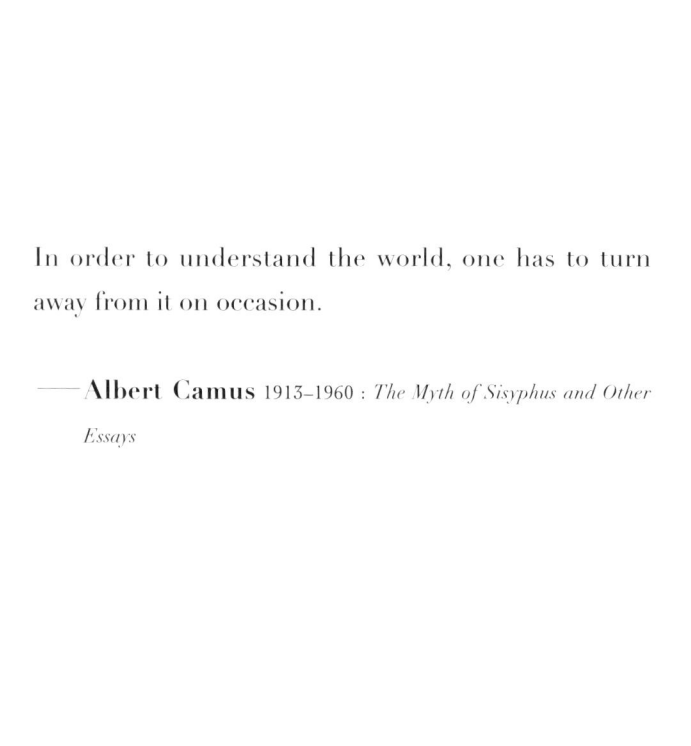

In order to understand the world, one has to turn away from it on occasion.

────**Albert Camus** 1913–1960 : *The Myth of Sisyphus and Other Essays*

為了瞭解這個世界，我們必須偶爾從中逃離。

—— 卡繆《薛西佛斯神話與其它散文》

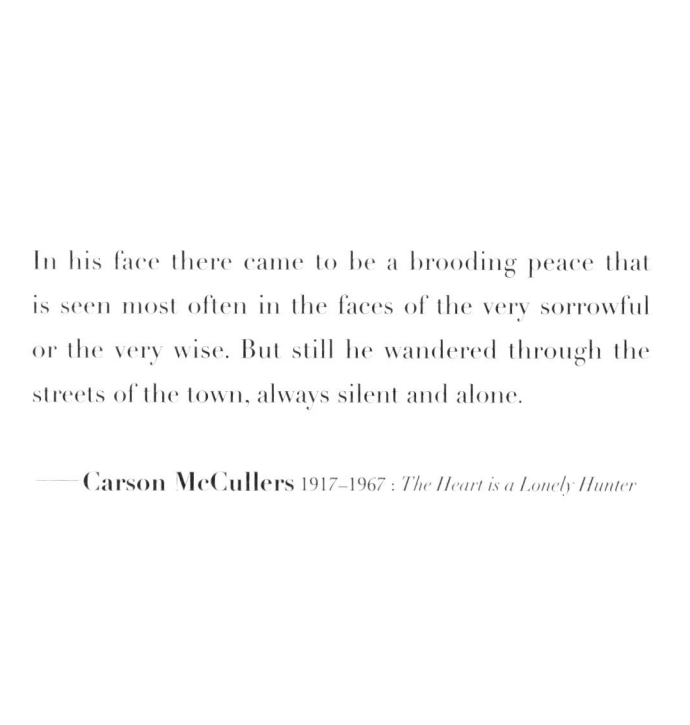

In his face there came to be a brooding peace that is seen most often in the faces of the very sorrowful or the very wise. But still he wandered through the streets of the town, always silent and alone.

——**Carson McCullers** 1917–1967 : *The Heart is a Lonely Hunter*

孤獨，一個人的狂歡

他的臉上所浮現的沉思、平靜，幾乎只存在於極度哀傷或極度睿智的人臉上。但他依然在城內街上穿梭，沉默與孤寂得一如往常。

—— **麥卡勒斯**《心是孤獨的獵手》

Solitude has seven skins; nothing gets through any more.

——**Friedrich Nietzsche** 1844–1900 : *Ecce Homo*

孤獨有七層外殼；萬物皆無法穿透。

—— 尼采《瞧！這個人》

I must stay alone and know that I am alone to contemplate and feel nature in full; I have to surrender myself to what encircles me, I have to merge with my clouds and rocks in order to be what I am. Solitude is indispensable for my dialogue with nature.

——**Caspar David Friedrich** 1744–1840 : *from memoirs of Vasily Zhukovsky*

我必須保持孤獨、並且知道我是孤獨的,如此才能全然地思忖自然、感受自然。我得臣服於我周圍的一切事物,與我的雲和岩石融為一體,以成為真正的我。在我與自然的對話中,孤獨不可或缺。

—— 德國畫家 **卡斯柏・大衛・腓德利希**

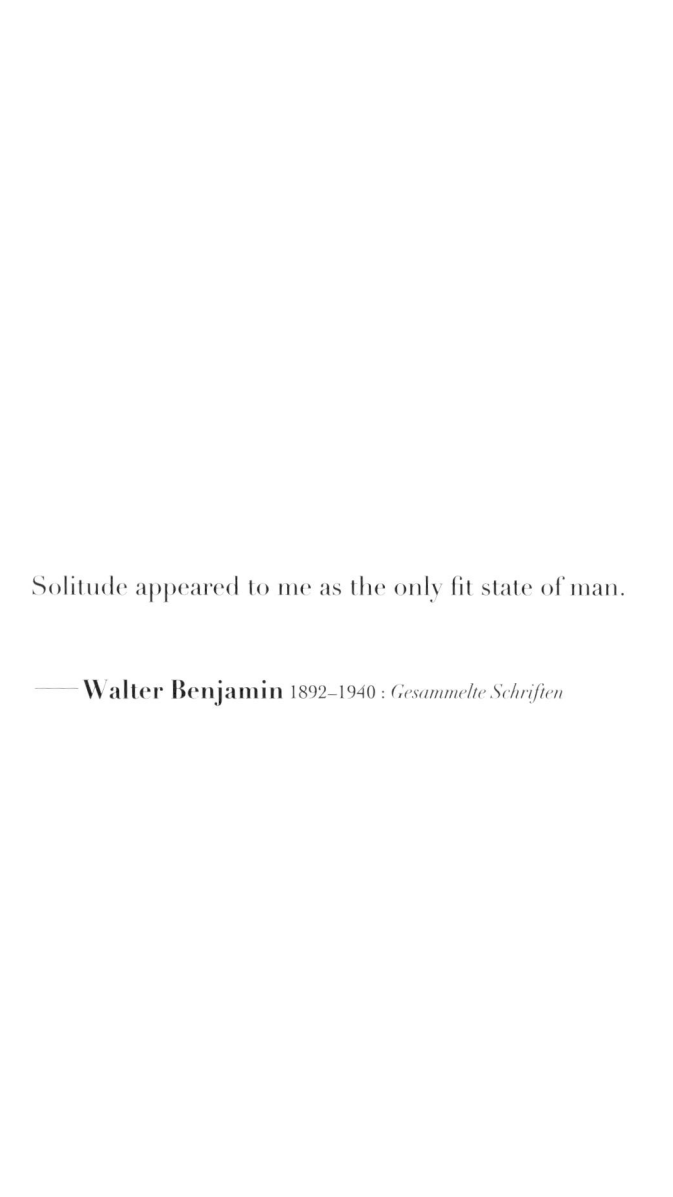

Solitude appeared to me as the only fit state of man.

—— **Walter Benjamin** 1892–1940 : *Gesammelte Schriften*

孤獨,一個人的狂歡

在我看來,孤獨是唯一適合人類的狀態。

—— **班雅明**《文集》

Solitude is the profoundest fact of the human condition. Man is the only being who knows he is alone, and the only one who seeks out another. His nature — if that word can be used in reference to man, who has 'invented' himself by saying 'no' to nature — consists in his longing to realize himself in another. Man is nostalgia and a search for communion. Therefore, when he is aware of himself he is aware of his lack of another, that is, of his solitude.

—— **Octavio Paz** 1914–1998 : *The Labyrinth of Solitude*

孤獨，　個人的狂歡

孤獨是對人類處境最深刻的陳述。人類是唯一知道自己孤單的物種，也是唯一會去尋找同伴的物種。他的天性——如果這個詞彙能用來形容藉由對天性說「不」而「創造」自我的人類——存在於他想從別人身上理解自我的渴望中。人類念舊、而且尋求交流，因此，當他意識到自己，也就意識到了自己缺乏的另一項東西，那就是他的孤獨。

——帕斯《孤獨的迷宮》

孤獨，一個人的狂歡

BOOK OF SOLITUDE

Death and birth are solitary experiences. We are born alone and we die alone. When we are expelled from the maternal womb, we begin the painful struggle that finally ends in death.

——**Octavio Paz** 1914–1998

死亡與誕生都是孤獨的經驗。我們生而孤獨，死亦孤獨，當我們被逐出母體子宮的那一刻，我們即展開一段將以死亡告終的痛苦掙扎。

──帕斯

Whosoever is delighted in solitude, is either a wild beast or a god.

—— **Francis Bacon** 1561–1626 : *Essays' XXVII* " *On Friendship* "

孤獨，一個人的狂歡

以孤獨為樂之人,若非野獸,便是神祇。

—— 培根《散文集》論友誼

The ingenious person will above all strive for freedom from pain and annoyance, for tranquility and leisure, and consequently seek a quiet, modest life, as undisturbed as possible, and accordingly, after some acquaintance with so–called human beings, choose seclusion and, if in possession of a great mind, even solitude. For the more somebody has in himself, the less he needs from the outside and the less others can be to him. Therefore, intellectual distinction leads to unsociability.

——**Arthur Schopenhauer** 1788–1860：*Parerga and Paralipomena*

有創造天分的人尤其會竭力追求免於苦痛和煩惱的自由，以及平靜和從容，因此他會尋求安靜、低調、盡可能不受侵擾的生活。也因此，在理解了所謂的人類之後，他會選擇離群索居；他若擁有偉大的心智，甚至會選擇孤獨。因為一個人倘若自我的內在越豐富，對於外界的需求也就越少，而他人對他的影響亦然。因此，智力上的差異會導致一個人不喜交際。

—— **叔本華**《附錄與補遺》

I have not a desire but a need for solitude.

——**Roland Barthes** 1915–1980 : *Mourning Diary*

孤獨，一個人的狂歡

我對孤獨並無渴求，只有需求。

―― **羅蘭・巴特**《哀悼日記》

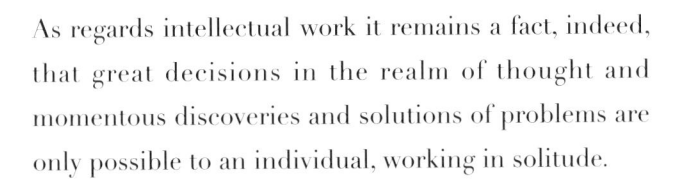

As regards intellectual work it remains a fact, indeed, that great decisions in the realm of thought and momentous discoveries and solutions of problems are only possible to an individual, working in solitude.

——**Sigmund Freud** 1856–1939 : *Group Psychology and the Analysis of the Ego*

至於需要運用智力的工作，這依然是個事實：的確，思想範疇上的重大決定、偉大發現和解決問題，這些都只有在個人獨自工作時才有可能發生。

—— 佛洛伊德《群體心理學與自我分析》

...solitude is not to be recommended to everyone, for you have to be strong in order to bear it and act alone.

―― **Paul Gauguin** 1848–1903 : *The Writings of a Savage*

孤獨，一個人的狂歡

孤獨不適合推薦給每個人，因為你必須夠堅強，才能忍受孤獨並單獨行動。

　　—— 高更《野人的書信》

The observations and encounters of a man of solitude and few words are at once more nebulous and more intense than those of a gregarious man, his thoughts more ponderable, more bizarre and never without a hint of sadness. Images and perceptions that might easily be dismissed with a glance, a laugh, an exchange of opinions occupy him unduly; they are heightened in the silence, gain in significance, turn into experience, adventure, emotion. Solitude begets originality, bold and disconcerting beauty, poetry.

——**Thomas Mann** 1875–1955 : *Death in Venice*

孤獨，一個人的狂歡

一個寡言孤獨者的觀察與遭遇,會比善於交際之人來得更難以理解,同時更為強烈;他的思慮更有價值、更奇特,而且往往帶著悲傷的痕跡。只消一個眼神、一個微笑或是一個意見交流就容易被遺忘的印象、感覺,會過度地占據他的思緒。它們在沉默裡茁壯、從意義中收穫,進而轉變為經驗、冒險與情感。孤獨會產生原創性、大膽與衝突之美和詩意。

──湯瑪斯・曼《魂斷威尼斯》

Isolation is a way to know ourselves.

———**Franz Kafka** 1883–1924

孤獨,一個人的狂歡

與世隔絕是認識自我之道。

──卡夫卡

All geniuses are peculiarly inclined to solitude, to which they are driven as much by their difference from others as the inner wealth with which they are quipped, since among humans, among diamonds, only the uncommonly great are suited as solitaires: the ordinary ones must be set in clusters to produce any effect.

—— **Arthur Schopenhauer** 1788–1860 : *On The Will In Nature*

孤獨，一個人的狂歡

因為與眾不同以及內在的天賦,所有的天才都格外具有孤獨的傾向。不論人類或是鑽石,只有非凡的極品才適合當隱士,而凡夫俗子只有群聚在一起才能有所作為。

—— 叔本華《論自然中的意志》

Every time a man (myself) gives way to vanity, every time he thinks and lives in order to show off, this is a betrayal. Every time, it has always been the great misfortune of wanting to show off which has lessened me in the presence of the truth. We do not need to reveal ourselves to others, but only to those we love. For then we are no longer revealing ourselves in order to seem but in order to give. There is much more strength in a man who reveals himself only when it is necessary. I have suffered from being alone, but because I have been able to keep my secret I have overcome the suffering of loneliness. To go right to the end implies knowing how to keep one's secret. And, today, there is no greater joy than to live alone and unknown.

——**Albert Camus** 1913–1960 : *Notebooks 1935-1942*

每當人（我自己）屈服於虛華，每當他為了炫耀而思考、生活，那就是一種背叛。想炫耀的念頭一直都是種不幸，讓我在真理面前萎縮。我們無須對他人揭露自我，只需向自己所愛的人袒露。因為此時的揭露自我，不再是為了呈現什麼，而是為了給予。只在必要時才展露自己的人更具力量。我深受孤獨所苦，但因為我能保守自己的祕密，我因而克服了孤獨的折磨。直到最後都不犯錯，正表示對保守祕密有所領略。在今日世界獨自生活與不為人知乃無上喜悅。

—— **卡繆**《卡繆札記 1935-1942》

I go, I go away, I walk, I wander, and everywhere I go I bear my shell with me, I remain at home in my room, among my books, I do not approach an inch nearer to Marrakech or Timbuktu. Even I took a train, a boat, or a motor—bus, if I went to Morocco for my holiday, if I suddenly arrived at Marrakech, I should be always in my room, at home. And if I walked in the squares and in the sooks, if I gripped an Arab's shoulder, to feel Marrakech in his person—well, that Arab would be at Marrakech, not I : I should still be seated in my room, placid and meditative as is my chosen life, two thousand miles away from the Moroccan and his burnoose. In my room. Forever.

—— **Jean-Paul Sartre** 1905–1980 : *The Age of Reason*

我前行，我遠離，我漫步，我流浪，凡所到之處，我都背著我的殼，我依然待在我的家裡，在我的書堆裡，我一步都沒有靠近馬拉喀什或廷巴克圖。就算我搭火車，搭船，搭巴士，就算我去摩洛哥度假，就算我突然抵達馬拉喀什，仍彷彿待在家中，我的房間裡。如果我去廣場散步，如果我攀著一個阿拉伯人的肩膀，感受他傳來的馬拉喀什氣息，嗯，身在馬拉喀什的，依然是那個阿拉伯人，不是我：我依舊坐在我的房間裡，如同我所選擇的平靜、充滿靈性的生活，遠離那個摩洛哥人與他的斗篷。在我的房間裡。永遠。

—— 沙特《理性時代》

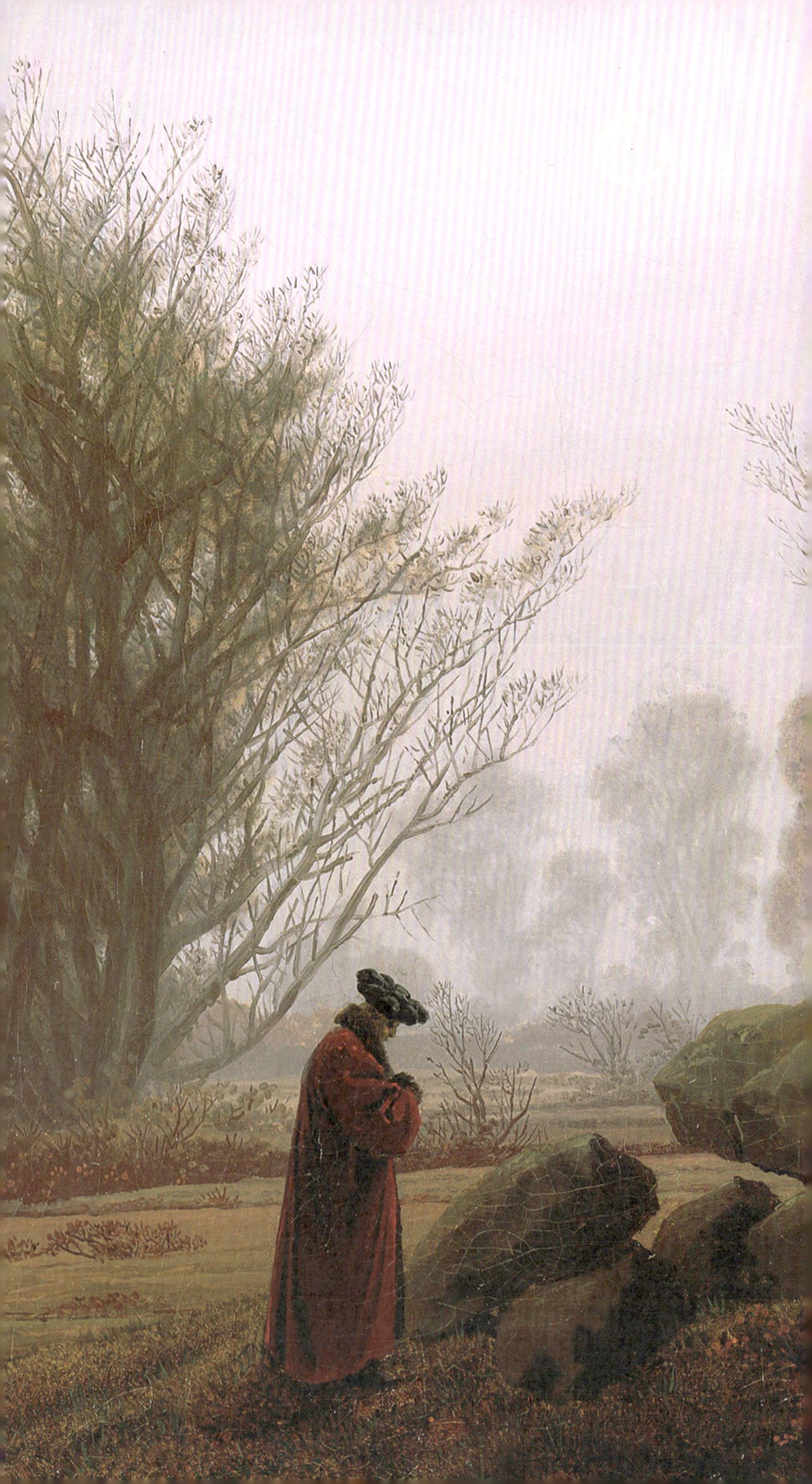

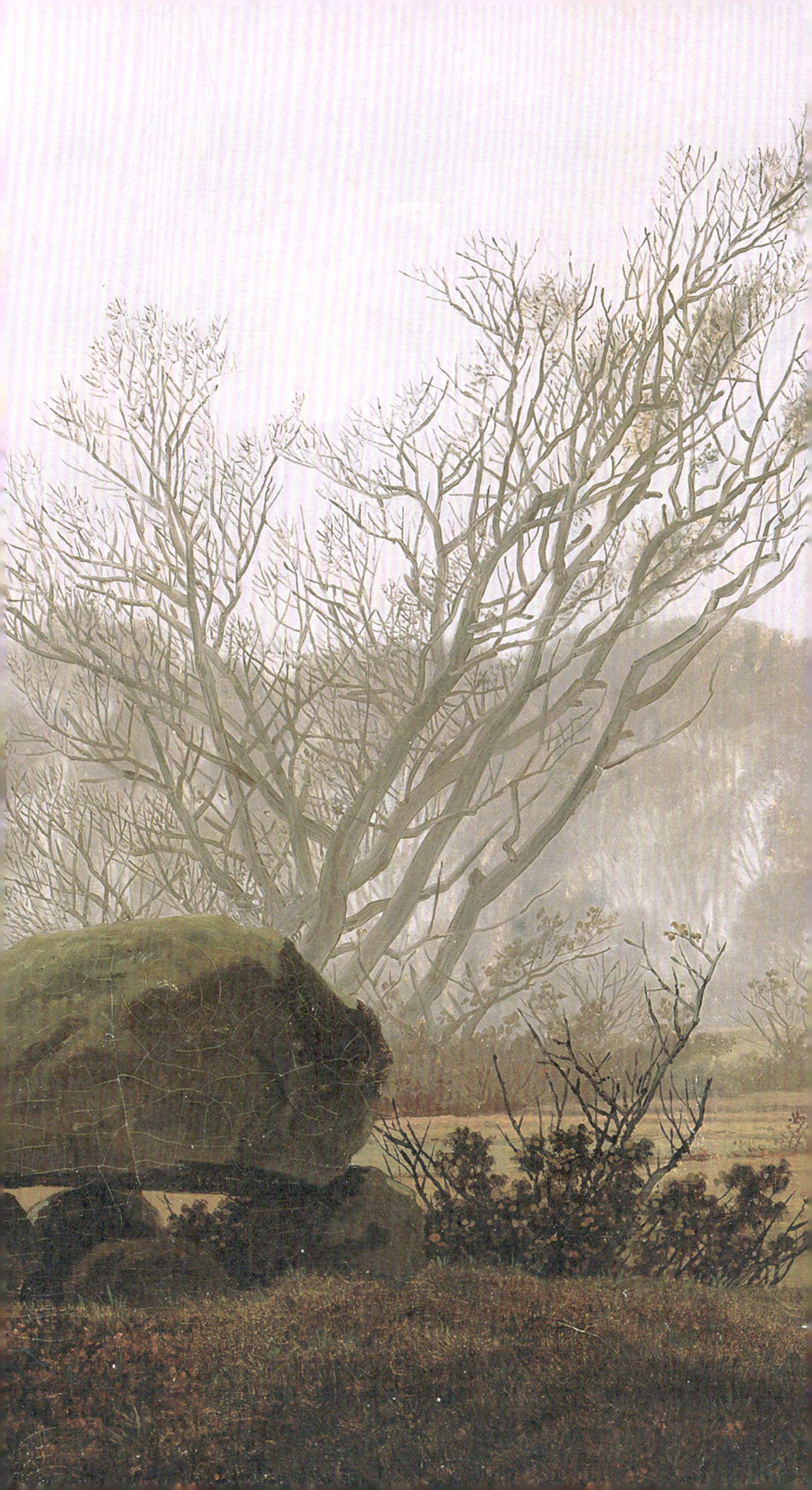

IV
灼傷，被猜疑的目光

A great fire burns within me, but no one stops to warm themselves at it, and passers-by only see a wisp of smoke.

———**Vincent van Gogh** 1850–1890 : *Letter*

孤獨，一個人的狂歡

我的靈魂暗藏炙熱烈火,卻無人駐足取暖,旁人走過只瞧見一縷輕煙。

—— 梵谷《書信集》

He was welcome everywhere he went, and was well-aware of his inability to tolerate solitude. He felt no inclination to be alone and avoided it as far as possible; he didn't really want to become any better acquainted with himself. He knew that if he wanted to show his talents to best advantage, he needed to strike sparks off other people to fan the flames of warmth and exuberance in his heart. On his own he was frosty, no use to himself at all, like a match left lying in its box.

——**Stefan Zweig** 1881–1942 : *The Burning Secret and Other Stories*

孤獨，一個人的狂歡

他所到之處無不受人歡迎，他也清楚地知道自己無法忍受孤獨。他無意獨處且對此敬而遠之，他一點都不想多了解自己一些。他知道如果他想讓自己的才能發揮到極致，他需要撲滅其他人的火花，來點燃他內心溫暖又豐沛的火焰。但他的內心已完全凍結，對他自己毫無用處，就如同一根靜靜躺在盒裡的火柴。

──**褚威格**《燃燒的祕密與其它故事》

孤獨,一個人的狂歡

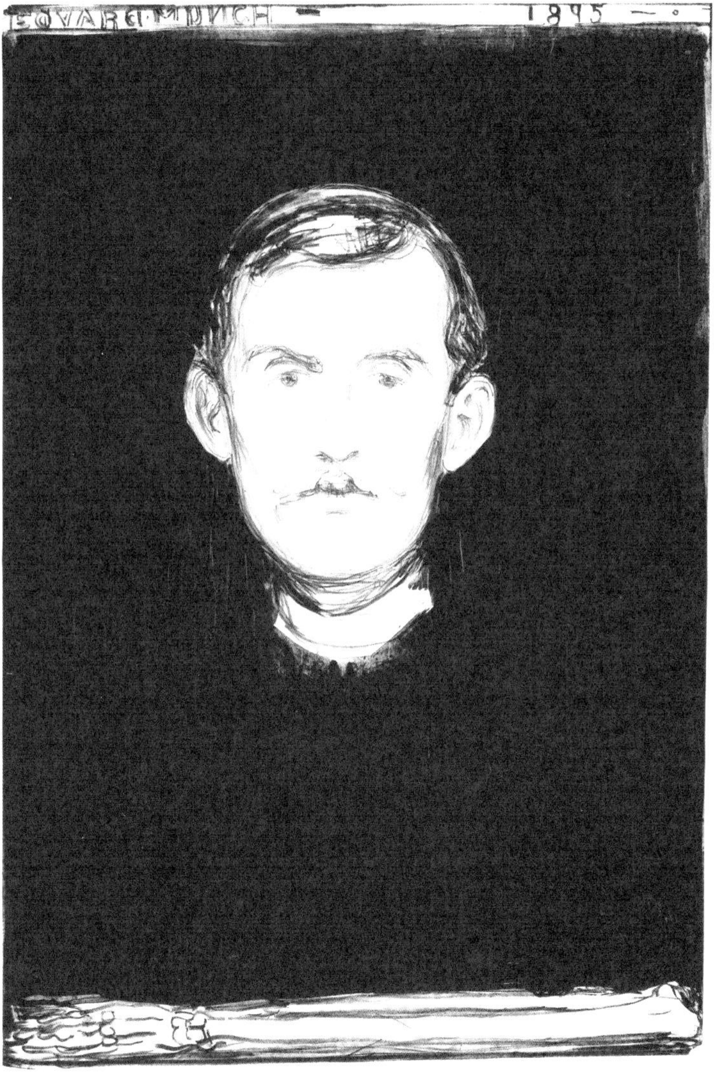
1895

I am alone, I thought, and they are everybody.

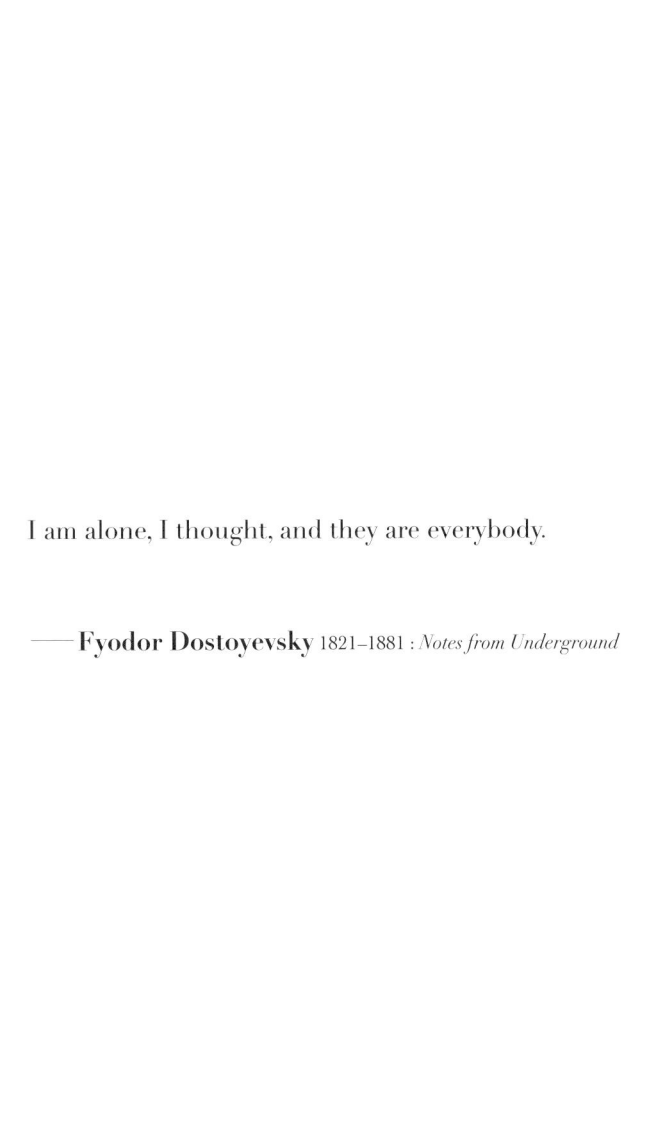

──**Fyodor Dostoyevsky** 1821–1881 : *Notes from Underground*

孤獨，一個人的狂歡

我想，我是孤獨的，所有人都與我不同。

──杜斯妥也夫斯基《地下室手記》

All great and precious things are lonely.

——**John Steinbeck** 1902–1968 : *East of Eden*

孤獨，一個人的狂歡

所有偉大與珍貴的事物都是寂寞的。

——約翰・史坦貝克《伊甸園東》

"Where are the people?" resumed the little prince at last. "It's a little lonely in the desert…"
"It is lonely when you're among people, too," said the snake.

——**Antoine de Saint-Exupéry** 1900–1944 : *The Little Prince*

孤獨，一個人的狂歡

「人都到哪去了呢？」小王子終於繼續說，「在沙漠裡還真有點寂寞⋯⋯」
「就算你在人群裡也一樣寂寞。」蛇說。

—— 聖修伯里《小王子》

God created man and, finding him not sufficiently alone, gave him a companion to make him feel his solitude more keenly.

―― **Paul Valéry** 1891–1980 : *Tel Quel*

上帝創造了人，發現他不夠孤單，於是給了他同伴，好讓他能更強烈地感受自己的孤獨。

──保羅・瓦勒里《如此》

We live, in fact, in a world starved for solitude, silence, and private: and therefore starved for meditation and true friendship.

—— **C.S. Lewis** 1898–1963 : *The Weight of Glory*

孤獨，一個人的狂歡

事實上，我們住在一個渴求孤獨、寂靜與隱私的世界，因此，我們渴望沉思與真實的友誼。

―― C.S. 路易斯《榮耀的重量》

What is the difference in being alone with another and being alone by one's self?

—— **Henrik Ibsen** 1828–1906

孤獨，一個人的狂歡

與他人同處時感到的孤單,跟與自己獨處時的孤獨有何不同?

—— 易卜生

Maybe ever'body in the whole damn world is scared of each other.

———**John Steinbeck** 1891–1980 : *Of Mice and Men*

孤獨，一個人的狂歡

也許在這個該死世上的每個人都懼怕彼此。

—— 史坦貝克《人鼠之間》

You talk when you cease to be at peace with your thoughts;
And when you can no longer dwell in the solitude of your heart you live in your lips, and sound is a diversion and a pastime.
And in much of your talking, thinking is half murdered.

—— **Kahlil Gibran** 1883–1931 : *The Prophet*

孤獨，一個人的狂歡

當你停止與你的思緒和平共處時,你開始說話。
當你再也無法安居於內心的孤獨,你住到你的唇上,
而聲音就是一種轉移,一種消遣。
在大多數的談話中,你的思考能力已被扼殺了一半。

──紀伯倫《先知》

What loneliness is more lonely than distrust?

——**George Eliot** 1819–1880 : *Middlemarch*

孤獨,一個人的狂歡

何種寂寞比猜疑更孤寂?

──喬治・艾略特《米德爾馬契》

I want to be with those who know secret things or else alone.

——**Rainer Maria Rilke** 1875–1926

我想要跟知道祕密的人在一起,不然寧可獨處。

—— 里爾克

One as deformed and horrible as myself, could not deny herself to me. My companion must be of the same species, and have the same defects... with whom I can live in the interchange of those sympathies necessary for my being...

—— **Mary Shelley** 1797–1851 : *Frankenstein*

孤獨,一個人的狂歡

醜陋可怕如我之人,就不會拒絕我。我的同伴一定要是我的同類,有著相同的缺陷,一個我和她可以活在彼此交換對如我族類之輩的必要同情之中的人。

——瑪麗‧雪萊《科學怪人》

We're all islands shouting lies to each other across seas of misunderstanding.

—— **Rudyard Kipling** 1865–1936 : *The Light That Failed*

我們是一座座隔著誤解之海、彼此大聲扯謊的島嶼。

—— 吉卜林《熄滅之燈》

Where solitude endeth, there beginneth the market-place; and where the market-place beginneth, there beginneth also the noise of the great actors, and the buzzing of the poison-flies.

—— **Friedrich Nietzsche** 1844–1900 : *Thus Spoke Zarathustra*

孤獨，一個人的狂歡

孤單結束之處,即是鬧市發源之地;而鬧市發源之地,亦是偉大演員們七嘴八舌與毒蠅嗡嗡作響的開端。

―― 尼采《查拉圖斯特拉如是說》

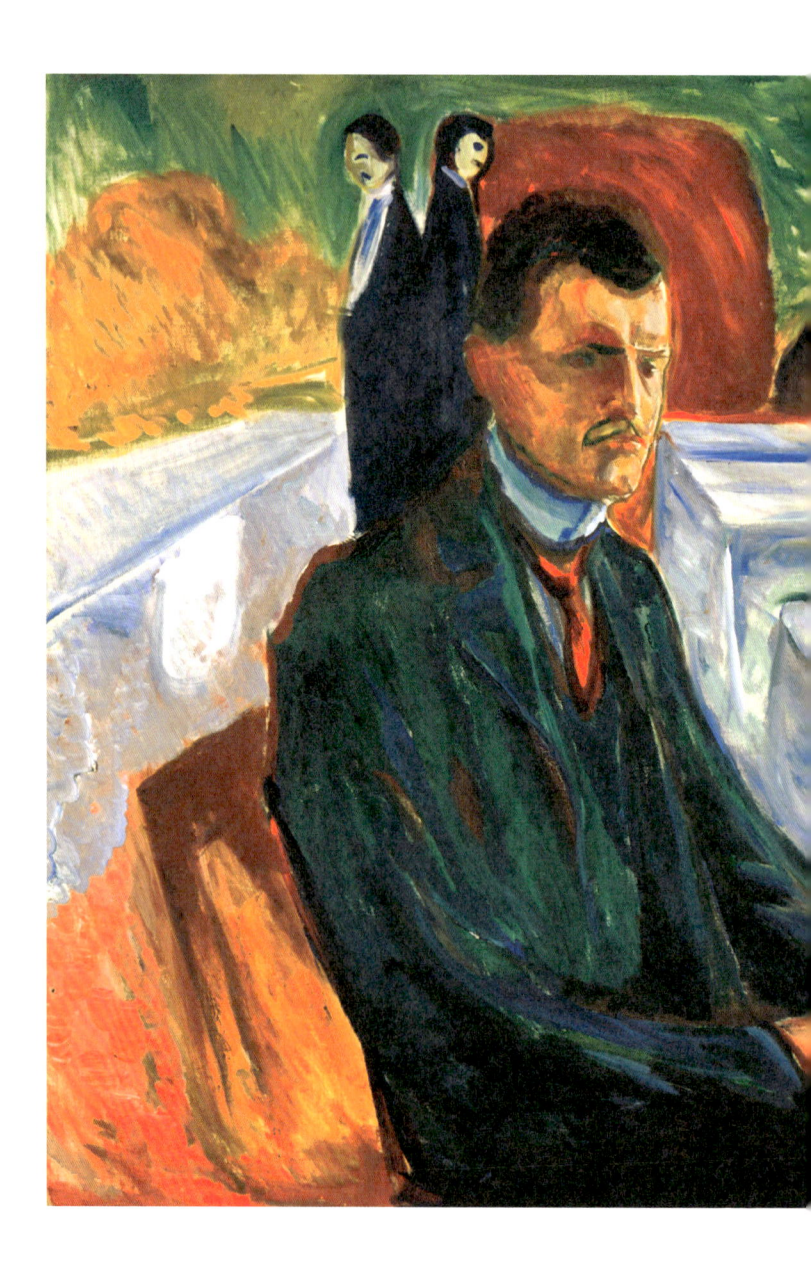

孤獨，一個人的狂歡

BOOK OF SOLITUDE

My loneliness was born when men praised my talkative faults and blamed my silent virtues.

—— **Kahlil Gibran** 1883–1931 : *Sand and Foam*

當人們盛讚我舌燦蓮花的罪過，譴責我默不作聲的美德時，我的寂寞油然而生。

──紀伯倫《沙與沫》

Life is an island in an ocean of solitude and seclusion.

Life is an island, rocks are its desires, trees its dreams, and flowers its loneliness, and it is in the middle of an ocean of solitude and seclusion.

Your life, my friend, is an island separated from all other islands and continents. Regardless of how many boats you send to other shores, you yourself are an island separated by its own pains, secluded its happiness and far away in its compassion and hidden in its secrets and mysteries.

I saw you, my friend, sitting upon a mound of gold, happy in your wealth and great in your riches and believing that a handful of gold is the secret chain that links the thoughts of the people with your own thoughts and links their feeling with your own.

I saw you as a great conqueror leading a conquering army toward the fortress, then destroying and capturing it.

On second glance I found beyond the wall of your treasures a heart trembling in its solitude and seclusion like the trembling of a thirsty man within a

孤獨，一個人的狂歡

生命是一座位處孤獨與隔絕之洋中的島嶼。

生命是一座島嶼,岩石是它的慾望,樹木是它的夢想,花朵是它的寂寞,而它就位處孤獨與隔絕之洋的中央。

你的人生是一座與其他島嶼和陸地分離的島,不論你派遣多少船隻駛向其他海岸,你自身就是一座被自己的痛苦隔離、隱藏自己的快樂、在自己的同情心中疏離、而且躲藏在自己的祕密與未解之謎中的島嶼。

我的朋友啊,我看見你坐在成堆的黃金上,在你的財富裡開心,在你的富裕裡偉大,而且相信,一把黃金便是將他人的想法與你自己的想法、他人的感受與你自己的感受鏈結為一的祕密鎖鏈。

我看見你,身為一位偉大的征服者,帶領著一隊遠征軍攻向堡壘,將之摧毀、占據。

第二眼,我看到在你以珍寶堆砌而成的那堵牆後,有一顆在孤獨與隔絕中顫抖的心,好似一個口渴的

cage of gold and jewels, but without water.

I saw you, my friend, sitting on a throne of glory surrounded by people extolling your charity, enumerating your gifts, gazing upon you as if they were in the presence of a prophet lifting their souls up into the planets and stars. I saw you looking at them, contentment and strength upon your face, as if you were to them as the soul is to the body.

On the second look I saw your secluded self standing beside your throne, suffering in its seclusion and quaking in its loneliness. I saw that self stretching its hands as if begging from unseen ghosts. I saw it looking above the shoulders of the people to a far horizon, empty of everything except its solitude and seclusion.

I saw you, my friend, passionately in love with a beautiful woman, filling her palms with your kisses as she looked at you with sympathy and affection in her eyes and sweetness of motherhood on her lips; I said, secretly, that love has erased his solitude and removed his seclusion and he is now within the eternal soul which draws toward itself, with love, those who were separated by solitude and seclusion.

人,雖身處在金銀珠寶築成的籠中,卻無水可喝。

我的朋友啊,我看見你坐在榮耀的權位上,身邊圍繞著頌揚你善行、細數你天賦的眾人,他們凝視你的目光,好似身在一個將他們的魂魄提升至日月星辰般高度的先知面前。我見到你望著他們,你的臉上盡是滿足與力量,彷若你之於他們正猶如靈魂之於軀體。

第二眼,我看到你隔絕的自己就站在你的權位旁邊,在自身的孤隱中受苦,在自己的孤寂中顫抖。我看見那個自己伸出雙手,好似在向不可見的鬼魂乞求。我看著那自己的目光越過他人肩膀,望向遠方,而那遠方的地平線上空無一物,唯有它自身的孤獨與隔絕。

我看見你,我的朋友啊,與一名美麗女子熱戀。當她眼帶同情與感情而雙唇充滿母愛甜美看著你時,你以吻填滿她的掌心。偷偷地,我說,那份愛抹去了他的孤獨,除去了他的寂寞,把他從孤獨與被人遺忘的處境帶回眾人之間。

On the second look I saw behind your soul another lonely soul, like a fog, trying in vain to become a drop of tears in the palm of that woman.

Your life, my friend, is a residence far away from any other residence and neighbors.

Your inner soul is a home far away from other homes named after you. If this residence is dark, you cannot light it with your neighbor's lamp; if it is empty you cannot fill it with the riches of your neighbor; were it in the middle of a desert, you could not move it to a garden planted by someone else.

Your inner soul, my friend, is surrounded with solitude and seclusion. Were it not for this solitude and this seclusion you would not be you and I would not be I. If it were not for that solitude and seclusion, I would, if I heard your voice, think myself to be speaking; yet, if I saw your face, i would imagine that I were looking into a mirror.

—— **Kahlil Gibran** 1883–1931 : *Mirrors of the Soul*

孤獨，一個人的狂歡

第二眼，我見到在你靈魂身後另一縷孤寂的靈魂，彷彿薄霧，想成為那女子掌心裡的一滴淚卻徒勞無功。

我的朋友，你的生命是個離群索居的宅邸。

你的內在靈魂是個與其他以你為名的家宅遙遙相隔的居所。如果這個居所一片漆黑，你無法藉鄰居的燈火照亮它；如果它空無一物，你無法利用鄰居的富饒來填滿它；它若位處沙漠中央，你無法將其移至其他人家的花園。

我的朋友啊，你的內在靈魂被孤獨與孤立包圍。若不是這份孤獨與這份孤立，你將不會是你，而我亦非我。若非那份孤獨與孤立，一旦我聽到你的聲音，我會以為那是我自己在說話；一旦我看見你的臉，我會以為我正望著一面鏡子。

——紀伯倫《靈魂之鏡》

The most terrible poverty is loneliness, and the feeling of being unloved.

—— **Mother Teresa** 1910–1997

孤寂與不被愛的感覺是最可怕的貧窮。

──德雷莎修女

If you are alone you belong entirely to yourself. If you are accompanied by even one companion you belong only half to yourself or even less in proportion to the thoughtlessness of his conduct and if you have more than one companion you will fall more deeply into the same plight.

—— **Leonardo da Vinci** 1452–1519 : *Notebook*

孤獨，一個人的狂歡

如果你獨自一人,你就全然屬於自己;如果你有朋友為伴,即使只有一個朋友,你也只有一半屬於自己,更可能因為他的魯莽行徑而降低屬於自己的比例;如果你有超過一個朋友,那你將陷入更糟糕的相同困境中。

—— 達文西《筆記》

Your bad love of yourselves makes solitude a prison to you.

—— Friedrich Nietzsche 1844–1900 : *Thus Spoke Zarathustra*

孤獨，一個人的狂歡

你們對自己變質的愛,讓孤獨成了你們自身的籠牢。

──尼采《查拉圖斯特拉如是說》

If you have a room which you do not want certain people to get into, put a lock on it for which they do not have the key. But there is no point in talking to them about it, unless of course you want them to admire the room from outside! The honorable thing to do is put a lock on the door which will be noticed only by those who can open it, not by the rest.

—— **Ludwig Wittgenstein** 1889–1951 : *Culture and Value*

孤獨，一個人的狂歡

如果你有一間不想讓特定人士進入的房間，就裝上一個他們沒有鑰匙能打開的鎖吧。但是跟他們談論這房間是沒有意義的，除非你希望他們從外頭欣賞它！最體面的方式，就是在門上裝上一個只有能打開門的人，而非其他人，才能察覺的鎖。

——維根斯坦《文化與價值》

If one's different, one's bound to be lonely.

———**Aldous Huxley** 1894–1963 : *Brave New World*

孤獨,一個人的狂歡

凡與眾不同者,其必也孤獨。

——**赫胥黎**《美麗新世界》

To retreat into oneself and meet nobody for hours on end — that is what one must be able to attain. To be alone, as one was alone as a child, when the grown-ups walked about involved in things which seemed great and important, because big people looked so busy and because one could comprehend nothing of their doings.

——**Rainer Maria Rilke** 1875–1926 : *Letters to a Young Poet*

回歸到孑然一身的狀態,且連續數小時都不與任何人見面,這是每個人必須具備的。當大人們四處參與看似偉大與重要的事情時,保持孤獨,孤獨得像是孩子,因為大人們向來忙碌,也因為他們無法被理解的作為。

—— 里爾克《給年輕詩人的信》

孤獨，一個人的狂歡

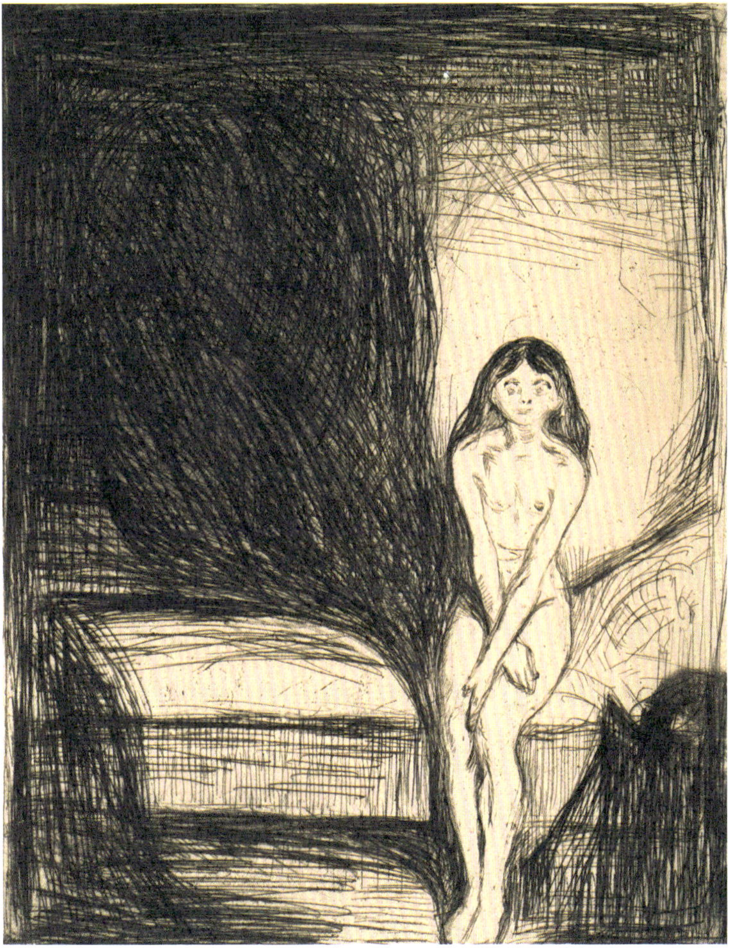

Deep down, the young are lonelier than the old.

—— **Anne Frank** 1929–1945 : *The Diary of a Young Girl*

孤獨，一個人的狂歡

內心深處，年輕人比老年人更寂寞。

—— 安妮・法蘭克《安妮日記》

Solitude sometimes is best society.

———**John Milton** 1608–1674 : *Paradise Lost*

孤獨,一個人的狂歡

孤獨有時是最佳的交際模式。

──約翰・密爾頓《失樂園》

So many people are shut up tight inside themselves like boxes, yet they would open up, unfolding quite wonderfully, if only you were interested in them.

——**Sylvia Plath** 1932–1963 : *Johnny Panic and the Bible of Dreams*

許多人將自己緊緊關入自身,彷彿盒子般。然而只要你對他們有興趣,他們就會美妙地攤展開來。

──普拉絲《強尼・潘尼克與夢想聖經》

孤獨,一個人的狂歡

BOOK OF SOLITUDE

V
說好一起寂寞

One evening he was in his room, his brow pressing hard against the pane, looking, without seeing them, at the chestnut trees in the park, which had lost much of their russet-coloured foliage. A heavy mist obscured the distance, and the night was falling grey rather than black, stepping cautiously with its velvet feet upon the tops of the trees. A great swan plunged and replunged amorously its neck and shoulders into the smoking water of the river, and its whiteness made it show in the darkness like a great star of snow. It was the single living being that somewhat enlivened the lonely landscape.

—— **Théophile Gautier** 1811–1872 : *Mademoiselle de Maupin*

一天傍晚，他在他房裡，眉毛緊貼著窗上玻璃，望著公園裡那些紅褐色枯葉已掉了一大半的栗子樹，但他視而不見。濃霧模糊了距離，與其說是黑，不如說是灰色的夜幕小心翼翼地步出絲絨般的雙足，踏上樹頂。一隻天鵝情意綿綿地將脖子和肩膀一再地伸入河上煙波，牠一身雪白有如黑暗中最明亮的一顆星。牠是唯一為這蕭瑟景致帶來生機的生物。

──戈蒂埃《莫班小姐》

We take our fetters with us; our freedom is not total: we still turn our gaze towards the things we have left behind; our imagination is full of them.

──**Michel de Montaigne** 1533–1592 : *On Solitude*

我們帶著羈絆隨行。我們並非全然自由，依舊不時回顧我們所遺棄之物，它們占據了我們全部的心思。

──蒙田《論孤獨》

He walked on in silence, the solitary sound of his footsteps echoing in his head, as in a deserted street, at dawn. His solitude was so complete, beneath a lovely sky as mellow and serene as a good conscience, amid that busy throng, that he was amazed at his own existence; he must be somebody else's nightmare, and whoever it was would certainly awaken soon.

——**Jean-Paul Sartre** 1905–1980 : *The Age of Reason*

孤獨，一個人的狂歡

他悄然走著，他孤獨的腳步聲迴盪在他的腦海裡，彷若在黎明，一條荒涼的街道上。他的孤獨如此完整，在宜人的天空下，寧靜、圓融得有如美好良知，在忙碌的群眾裡，他驚愕於自己的存在。他必定是某人的夢魘，而不管某人是誰，不久後都即將驚醒。

——沙特《理性時代》

Perhaps only people who are capable of real togetherness have that look of being alone in the universe. The others have a certain stickiness, they stick to the mass.

―― **D.H. Lawrence** 1885–1930 : *Lady Chatterley's Lover*

孤獨，一個人的狂歡

也許只有那些能夠真正團結的人,才會有那種遺世獨立的表情。而具相當依賴性的其他人,他們才會成群結隊。

——D.H. 勞倫斯《查泰萊夫人的情人》

Listen: I am ideally happy. My happiness is a kind of challenge. As I wander along the streets and the squares and the paths by the canal, absently sensing the lips of dampness through my worn soles, I carry proudly my ineffable happiness. The centuries will roll by, and schoolboys will yawn over the history of our upheavals; everything will pass, but my happiness, dear, my happiness will remain, in the moist reflection of a street lamp, in the cautious bend of stone steps that descend into the canal's black waters, in the smiles of a dancing couple, in everything with which God so generously surrounds human loneliness.

———**Vladimir Nabokov** 1899–1977 : *Selected Letters, 1940-1977*

孤獨，一個人的狂歡

聽著：我無比快樂。我的快樂是一種挑戰。當我沿著街道、廣場和運河旁的小徑漫步時，不經意地感受到鞋底傳來的濕氣，我驕傲地帶著我無以名狀的快樂。世代將會變遷，學子們對於我們崛起的歷史亦會興趣缺缺，萬物終歸於過去，但是我的快樂，親愛的，我的快樂必會留存，留存在微濕的街燈倒影中，留存在延伸至運河黑色流水中的石階上，留存在舞者的笑靨裡，留存在被上天慷慨賜與每個人的孤寂所包圍的萬物裡。

——納博科夫《書信選 1940－1977》

I care for myself. The more solitary, the more friendless, the more unsustained I am, the more I will respect myself.

——**Charlotte Brontë** 1816–1855 : *Jane Eyre*

我喜歡自己。越是孤獨，越是沒有朋友，越是孤立無援，我就越尊敬自己。

—— 夏綠蒂・勃朗特《簡愛》

孤獨，一個人的狂歡

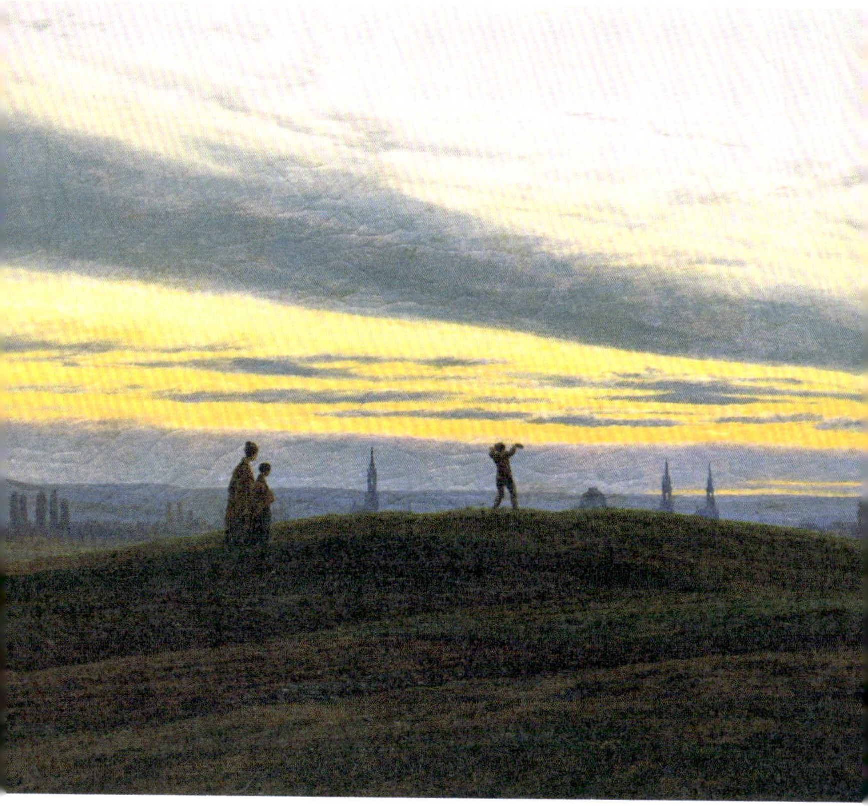

The solitary speaks. "One receives as a reward for much ennui, ill-humour and boredom, such as a solitude without friends, books, duties or passions must entail, one harvests those quarters of an hour of the deepest immersion in oneself and nature. He who completely entrenches himself against boredom also entrenches himself against himself: he will never get to drink the most potent refreshing draught from the deepest well of his own being."

—— **Friedrich Nietzsche** 1844–1900 : *Human, All Too Human*

這個隱居者說話了。「人們將之當作無聊不堪、低級幽默及可憎事物的獎賞，例如，一個隱居者必須承擔沒有朋友、書本、職責或熱情的風險，來取得零碎時間融入自己與大自然最深處。完全將自己阻隔在無聊事物之外的人，同樣也將自己阻隔在自身之外——他將永遠無法嘗到，從他自身之井的最深處汩汩湧出，那最有效、最清新的瓊漿玉液。」

——尼采《人性，一切都太人性》

Solitude is indeed dangerous for a working intelligence. We need to have around us people who think and speak. When we are alone for a long time we people the void with phantoms.

——**Guy de Maupassant** 1850–1893：*Le Horla et Autres Contes Fantastiques*

孤獨，一個人的狂歡

孤獨對於運行中的智慧而言確實危險，我們身邊需要有會思考與說話的人。當我們孤單太久，我們將如行屍走肉。

―― 莫泊桑《奧爾拉與其他癡人說夢》

Find meaning. Distinguish melancholy from sadness. Go out for a walk. It doesn't have to be a romantic walk in the park, spring at its most spectacular moment, flowers and smells and outstanding poetical imagery smoothly transferring you into another world. It doesn't have to be a walk during which you'll have multiple life epiphanies and discover meanings no other brain ever managed to encounter. Do not be afraid of spending quality time by yourself. Find meaning or don't find meaning but 'steal' some time and give it freely and exclusively to your own self. Opt for privacy and solitude. That doesn't make you antisocial or cause you to reject the rest of the world. But you need to breathe. And you need to be.

——**Albert Camus** 1913–1960 : *Notebooks 1951-1959*

找出意義。辨別出哀愁與悲傷的差異。出去散個步吧。那不必是公園裡的浪漫散步，在春光明媚的時節，讓繁花、香氣與充滿詩意的意境，巧妙地將你帶往另一個世界；那不必是個得從中獲得多重頓悟與發現無人能領悟之意義的散步。勿懼怕花費珍貴的時光跟自己相處。重點不在於找意義與否，而是要「偷」些時間，讓它自由，而且專屬於你。選擇隱密與獨處，這不會讓你反社會，或是導致你拒絕世上的其他人；但是你需要呼吸，而且你必須這麼做。

——卡繆《卡繆札記 1951-1959》

It is a very strange sensation to inexperience youth to feel itself quite alone the world, cut adrift from every connection, uncertain whether the port to which it is bound can be reached, and prevented by many impediments from returning to that it has quitted. The charm of adventure sweetens that sensation, the glow of pride warms it; but then the throb of fear disturbs it; and fear with me became predominant when half an hour elapsed, and still I was alone.

——**Charlotte Brontë** 1816–1855 : *Jane Eyre*

對未經世事的年輕人而言,體會隻身孤獨於世是種奇異的感受。斷絕所有聯繫,漫無目的地漂流,不確定能否抵達與其相羈絆的港口,而且重重障礙阻撓著復返本已離開的所在。冒險的魅力甜美了這番感受,驕傲的光芒將之溫暖,但隨之而來的恐懼卻擾亂了它,半小時過去,我揮之不去的恐懼主宰了一切,而我依然孤獨。

──夏綠蒂・勃朗特《簡愛》

We carry about us the burden of what thousands of people have said and the memories of all our misfortunes. To abandon all that is to be alone, and the mind that is alone is not only innocent but young—not in time or age, but young, innocent, alive at whatever age—and only such a mind can see that which is truth and that which is not measurable by words.

——**Jiddu Krishnamurti** 1895–1986 : *Freedom from the Known*

我們將數以千計的人說過的話，與我們所有不幸的回憶，全扛在肩上。唯有孤獨才能拋開這一切。孤獨的心靈不僅單純，而且年輕 —— 這並非指歲月或年紀，而是在各個年紀都能年輕、天真、活躍 —— 唯有這樣的心靈才能看清何者為真，及那些無法以言語度量的事實。

—— 克里希那穆提《從已知中解脫》

Guard well your spare moments. They are like uncut diamonds. Discard them and their value will never be known. Improve them and they will become the brightest gems in a useful life.

———**Ralph Waldo Emerson** 1803–1882

善加守護你的空閒時光。它們就像未經切割的鑽石，棄置它們，它們的價值將永被埋沒；仔細雕琢，它們將會成為有用的人生中最璀璨的寶石。

──愛默生

But for pain words are lacking. There should be cries, cracks, fissures, whiteness passing over chintz covers, interference with the sense of time, of space; the sense also of extreme fixity in passing objects; and sounds very remote and then very close; flesh being gashed and blood spurting, a joint suddenly twisted—beneath all of which appears something very important, yet remote, to be just held in solitude.

——**Virginia Woolf** 1882–1941 : *The Waves*

但是用來形容痛苦的詞彙就很缺乏。應該要有能夠表現哭泣、裂痕、分裂、印花棉布封面上的白色痕跡、時間感與空間感的干擾、變動之物體的永久固定感、遠距離的聲音與近距離的聲音、皮開肉綻、鮮血直流、突然關節扭傷——在這些之下，顯現出某事十分重要，卻很遙遠，只能在孤獨裡發生。

—— 吳爾芙《海浪》

Let this little book be thy friend, if, owing to fortune or through thine own fault, thou canst not find a dearer companion.

——**Johann Wolfgang von Goethe** 1749–1832 : *The Sorrows of Young Werther*

如果，因為命運或是你自己的錯誤，使你找不到更親愛的夥伴，那就讓這本小書成為你的朋友吧。

—— 歌德《少年維特的煩惱》

Solitude is precious balm to my heart in these paradistic parts.

——**Johann Wolfgang von Goethe** 1749–1832 : *The Sorrows of Young Werther*

在這些天堂般的情境裡，孤獨是我心靈珍貴的慰藉品。

—— 歌德《少年維特的煩惱》

孤獨，一個人的狂歡

BOOK OF SOLITUDE

Reading is that fruitful miracle of a communication in the midst of solitude.

—— **Marcel Proust** 1877–1922

孤獨，一個人的狂歡

閱讀是在孤獨之中，豐饒的溝通奇蹟。

—— 普魯斯特

Who hears music, feels his solitude
Peopled at once.

——**Robert Browning** 1812–1889 : *The Complete Poetical Works of Browning*

孤獨,一個人的狂歡

聽得音樂,感覺自身的孤獨,
就是曾經身而為人的證明。

──羅伯特・白朗寧《白朗寧詩集全選》

I love the dark hours of my being.
My mind deepens into them.
There I can find, as in old letters,
the days of my life, already lived,
and held like a legend, and understood.

——**Rainer Maria Rilke** 1875–1926 : *Rilke's Book of Hours: Love Poems to God*

我愛我自己的黑暗時光

我的思緒深入它們。

在那裡,如同陳舊的信件中,我可以尋得

已經活過的,如同傳奇般的,被理解的那些

我的生命歲月。

—— **里爾克**《里爾克的時光之書:獻給上帝的詩》

Go oft to the house of thy friend, for weeds choke the unused path.

―― **Ralph Waldo Emerson** 1803–1882

孤獨,　一個人的狂歡

多去你朋友家中走走吧,雜草已讓這沒人走動的小徑窒息了。

──愛默生

No man is an island, entire of itself; every man is a piece of the continent, a part of the main. If a clod be washed away by the sea, Europe is the less, as well as if a promontory were, as well as if a manor of thy friend's or of thine own were: any man's death diminishes me, because I am involved in mankind, and therefore never send to know for whom the bells tolls; it tolls for thee.

——**John Donne** 1572–1631 : *No Man Is An Island*

沒有人是一座孤島，全然屬於自己；
每個人都是陸地的一隅，整體的一部分。
如果海水沖走一方泥塊，歐洲就會變小；
一塊峽角如是，你或你友人的莊園亦如是。
任何一個人的死亡都會帶走我的一部分，
因為我與人類息息相關，
因此，別問那喪鐘為誰而鳴，它為你而鳴。

── 約翰・多恩《沒有人是一座孤島》

It's no good trying to get rid of your own aloneness. You've got to stick to it all your life. Only at times, at times, the gap will be filled in. At times! But you have to wait for the times. Accept your own aloneness and stick to it, all your life. And then accept the times when the gap is filled in, when they come. But they've got to come. You can't force them.

—— **D.H. Lawrence** 1885–1930 : *Lady Chatterley's Lover*

試著擺脫你自身的孤獨是沒有好處的，你一生都要與之共處。只有偶爾，偶爾，這道鴻溝會被填滿。偶爾！然而你必須等待時機到來。你要接納自己的孤獨並與之共處，一輩子都是。當填滿鴻溝的時機來臨，你要接受；然而時機自有運行之道，你無法強求。

—— D.H. 勞倫斯《查泰萊夫人的情人》

Solitude is a virtue for us, since it is a sublime inclination and impulse to cleanliness which shows that contact between people, "society" inevitably makes things unclean. Somewhere, sometime, every community makes people—base.

——**Friedrich Nietzsche** 1844–1900 : *Beyond Good and Evil*

孤獨對我們而言是一種美德，因為它是一種對於潔淨絕對的傾向與衝動；這種潔淨彰顯出「社會」這種無可避免、並使事物不潔的人際交流方式。某處，某時，每個社群都使得人們──平庸。

──尼采《超越善惡》

We must become so alone, so utterly alone, that we withdraw into our innermost self. It is a way of bitter suffering. But then our solitude is overcome, we are no longer alone, for we find that our innermost self is the spirit, that it is God, the indivisible. And suddenly we find ourselves in the midst of the world, yet undisturbed by its multiplicity, for our innermost soul we know ourselves to be one with all being.

—— **Hermann Hesse** 1877–1962 : *Reflections*

孤獨，一個人的狂歡

我們必須變得如此孤獨，全然地孤獨，使我們退縮至最深處的自我之中。這是一個痛苦的折磨。然而，我們征服了孤獨，我們再也不孤單，因為我們發現，最深處的自我就是我們的靈魂，就是上帝，無法切割。剎時，我們發現自己身在世界的中央，卻不受它的多樣紛雜所擾，因為我們最深處的靈魂知道，我們必與萬物合而為一。

—— 赫塞《反思集》

孤獨，一個人的狂歡

BOOK OF SOLITUDE

I live in that solitude which is painful in youth, but delicious in the years of maturity.

——Albert Einstein 1879–1955

孤獨，一個人的狂歡

我活在那年少時令我痛苦萬分，但在成熟年歲裡卻倍感豐饒甜美的孤寂當中。

──愛因斯坦

In spite of language, in spite of intelligence and intuition and sympathy, one can never really communicate anything to anybody. The essential substance of every thought and feeling remains incommunicable, locked up in the impenetrable strong-room of the individual soul and body. Our life is a sentence of perpetual solitary confinement.

—— **Aldous Huxley** 1894–1963

儘管有語言、智力、直覺和同情心,人依然無法真正與任何人溝通任何事。每項思緒與感受的必要本質依然無法交流,都像是禁錮在個人的靈魂與軀體那無法穿透的保險庫中。人生就是一記永遠孤獨幽禁的判決。

—— 赫胥黎

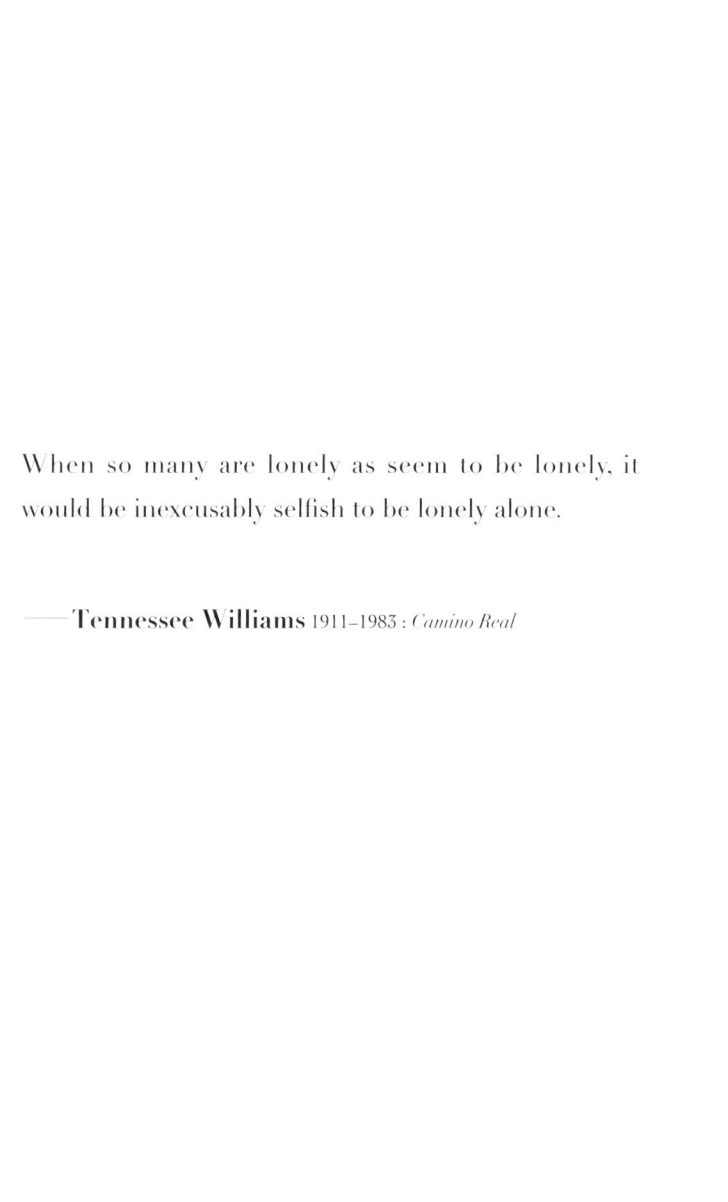

When so many are lonely as seem to be lonely, it would be inexcusably selfish to be lonely alone.

——**Tennessee Williams** 1911–1983 : *Camino Real*

孤獨, 一個人的狂歡

當這麼多的人為了看起來寂寞而寂寞，獨自地寂寞就是不可饒恕的自私。

──田納西・威廉斯《皇家大路》

Human beings must love something, and, in the dearth of worthier objects of affection, I contrived to find a pleasure in loving and cherishing a faded graven image, shabby as a miniature scarecrow. It puzzles me now to remember with what absurd sincerity I doated on this little toy, half fancying it alive and capable of sensation. I could not sleep unless it was folded in my night-gown; and when it lay there safe and warm, I was comparatively happy, believing it to be happy likewise.

—— **Charlotte Brontë** 1816–1855 : *Jane Eyre*

人類必定有所愛之物。因此,在缺乏更有價值的愛慕之物的情況下,我設法從喜愛與珍惜一只破舊如小稻草人的褪色人偶中找到樂趣。如今,我已記不得,對這個小玩物我當初付出了何等荒謬的真心。我幻想它活生生、而且有知覺;若沒將它覆蓋在我的睡袍下,我便無法成眠;而當它寧靜安詳地躺著,我心中便一陣欣喜,深信它也一樣高興。

——夏綠蒂・勃朗特《簡愛》

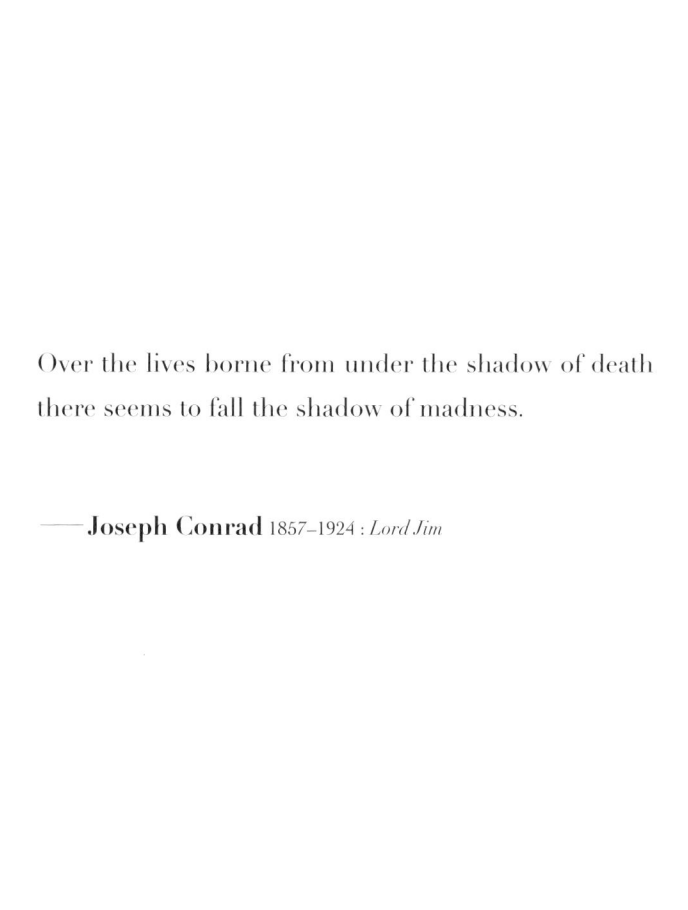

Over the lives borne from under the shadow of death there seems to fall the shadow of madness.

——**Joseph Conrad** 1857–1924 : *Lord Jim*

越過從死亡陰影下誕生的生命，似乎又墜入了瘋狂的陰影。

——康拉德《吉姆爺》

I gang my own gait and have never belonged to my country, my home, my friends, or even my immediate family, with my whole heart; in the face of all these ties I have never lost an obstinate sense of detachment, of the need for solitude — a feeling which increases with the years.

——**Albert Einstein** 1879–1955 : *The World As I See It*

我全心全意以自己的步伐前行，我從不屬於我的國家、我的家庭、我的朋友、甚至我最親密的家人。在這些羈絆面前，我從未失去對於疏離和孤獨的頑固堅持──這是一種隨年齡而增長的感受。

──愛因斯坦《我所看見的世界》

That's love: Two lonely persons keep each other safe and touch each other and talk to each other.

——**Rainer Maria Rilke**

孤獨，一個人的狂歡

兩個寂寞的人彼此保護，彼此撫觸，彼此交談 ——
這就是愛。

—— 里爾克

孤獨，一個人的狂歡

ILLUSTRATIONS

Jacket: *Nighthawks* (1942), Edward Hopper
Cover: *The Monk by the Sea* (1809), Caspar David Friedrich

I.
1. *The Kiss* (1895), Edvard Munch
2. *Eva Mudocci* (1903), Edvard Munch
3. *The Lonely Ones* (1896), Edvard Munch
4. *Separation* (1896), Edward Munch
5. *Two Women on the Beach* (1898), Edvard Munch
6. *Consolation* (1894), Edvard Munch
7. *Love and Pain* (1894), Edvard Munch

II.
1. *Separation* (1896), Edvard Munch
2. *Woman on the Stairs* (1825), Caspar David Friedrich
3. *Melancholy* (1896), Edvard Munch
4. *Jealousy* (1907), Edvard Munch

III.
1. *The Chasseur in the Forest* (1814), Caspar David Friedrich
2. *Wanderer above the Sea of Fog* (1818), Caspar David Friedrich
3. *The Morning* (1821), Caspar David Friedrich
4. *Winter Landscape* (1811), Caspar David Friedrich
5. *Woman before the Setting Sun* (1819), Caspar David Friedrich
6. *A Walk at the Dusk* (1830-35), Caspar David Friedrich

IV.
1. *Self-Portrait with Cigarette* (1895), Edvard Munch
2. *Self-Portrait* (1895), Edvard Munch
3. *Self-Portrait with a Bottle of Wine* (1906), Edvard Munch
4. *Despair* (1894), Edvard Munch
5. *Puberty* (1902), Edvard Munch
6. *Inger on the Beach* (1889), Edvard Munch

V.
1. *Moonrise over the Sea* (1822), Caspar David Friedrich
2. *The Evening Star* (1830), Caspar David Friedrich
3. *Brothers* (1835), Caspar David Friedrich
4. *Moonrise by the Sea* (1822), Caspar David Friedrich
5. *Two Men Contemplating the Moon* (1825-30), Caspar David Friedrich
6. *The Kiss* (1897), Edvard Munch

孤獨，一個人的狂歡

孤獨，一個人的狂歡

作者／卡夫卡、尼采、吳爾芙……等人
譯者／黃意雯

總編輯／富察
主編／林家任
執編／楊沱、楊樺
企劃／蔡慧華

排版／宸遠彩藝
設計／井十二設計研究室

出版／八旗文化・遠足文化事業股份有限公司
發行／遠足文化事業股份有限公司
　　　（讀書共和國出版集團）
地址／新北市新店區民權路 108-2 號 9 樓
電話／02.2218.1417
傳真／02.2218.8057
客服專線／0800.221.029
信箱／gusa0601@gmail.com

法律顧問／華洋法律事務所 蘇文生律師
印刷／通南彩色印刷股份有限公司
出版日期／2016 年 11 月／初版一刷
　　　　　2025 年 10 月／初版十一刷
定價／350 元

孤獨，一個人的狂歡
齊克果等著；黃意雯譯
初版・新北市
八旗文化，遠足文化，2016.11
320 面；13 × 21 公分
ISBN 978-986-93562-7-5（平裝）

1. 哲學　2. 文集

107
105018914

Complex Chinese translation © 2016 by Gusa Press, a Division of Walkers Cultural Enterprises Ltd.

◎版權所有，翻印必究。本書如有缺頁、破損、裝訂錯誤，請寄回更換
◎歡迎團體訂購，另有優惠。請電洽業務部（02）22181417 分機 1124、1135
◎本書言論內容，不代表本公司／出版集團之立場或意見，文責由作者自行承擔